STUDY ABROAD
A PARENT'S GUIDE

For Parents of College and University Students

Contemplating a Study Abroad Experience

by William W. Hoffa

NAFSA
ASSOCIATION OF
INTERNATIONAL
EDUCATORS

About the Author William W. Hoffa holds academic degrees from Michigan, Harvard, and Wisconsin. He has been a professor of English and American Studies at Vanderbilt University and Hamilton College, as well as a Senior Fulbright Lecturer at the University of Jyvaskyla, Finland (1974–75) and a National Endowment for the Humanities Fellow at the University of New Mexico (1978–79). He now teaches in the Master's in International and Intercultural Management program at the School for International Training in Brattleboro, Vermont.

Since 1981 Hoffa has been a full-time international educator based in Amherst, Massachusetts. Well known in the field of international education for his years as a leader within NAFSA: Association of International Educators, he has held positions with the Council on International Educational Exchange and Scandinavian Seminar, Inc.,

 and is the author or editor of many essays, interviews, and reports on education abroad, including "The Student Guide to Study Abroad," for studyabroad.com, and *NAFSA's Guide to Education Abroad for Advisers and Administrators* (1997, coedited with John Pearson). An overview of his current activities for Academic Consultants International is available at www.academic-consultants.com.

He is the father of two children: a daughter who studied abroad and a son who did not.

Photograph courtesy of the *Daily Hampshire Gazette*, Northampton, Mass.

About NAFSA

NAFSA: Association of International Educators promotes the exchange of students and scholars to and from the United States. The Association sets and upholds standards of good practice and provides professional education and training that strengthen institutional programs and services related to international educational exchange. NAFSA provides a forum for discussion of issues and a network for sharing information as it seeks to increase awareness of and support for international education in higher education, in government, and in the community.

NAFSA's members—numbering more than 8,000 university administrators and community volunteers from all 50 states and 60 countries—share a belief that international educational exchange advances learning and scholarship, builds respect among different peoples, and encourages constructive leadership in a global community.

A majority of NAFSA's members can be found on college and university campuses working as study abroad advisers, foreign student advisers, admissions officers, directors of international programs, and administrators of intensive English programs.

Nearly all of the 90,000 American students who study abroad each year are enrolled at the two thousand postsecondary institutions served by NAFSA members.

NAFSA also draws members from associations and foundations, international and national corporations, community organizations, overseas educational advising centers, and cultural groups. The embassies and consulates of more than 160 countries participate in NAFSA activities as international affiliates.

Helping students and scholars from diverse educational and cultural backgrounds to make the most of a stay outside their home country requires special knowledge and competencies. NAFSA members foster optimal exchange experiences by anticipating and responding to the needs of students engaged in the unique and challenging experience of crossing borders to study.

NAFSA: Association of International Educators
1875 Connecticut Avenue N.W., Suite 1000
Washington, DC 20009-5728 USA
Tel: 202-462-4811, Fax: 202-667-3419
Internet: inbox@nafsa.org, http://www.nafsa.org

ISBN 0-912207-78-7

Printed in the United States of America
4 3 2 1   00 01 99 98

Designed and produced by Meadows Design Office Incorporated, Washington, D.C.
Cover photograph by Bob Handelman Images, New York, N.Y.

Contents

Introduction

This is the first full-length book to provide an overview of study abroad for parents. You are to be applauded for taking the time to learn about this powerful educational experience. Armed with your new knowledge, you will be able to offer your child, now a young adult, not only your love and understanding, but also an informed perspective.

The premise of the book is that there are many reasons why parents and students should consider study abroad. Enriching undergraduate degree studies and preparing for life and work in our increasingly interdependent world are only two of those reasons. Having said this, it is also the case that study abroad is not for everyone, and so for some students it may not be the wisest choice, especially if what they miss by not being on campus is ultimately more important to their education than what they can learn through studying overseas. The choice of whether or not to study abroad depends on becoming informed about what a study abroad experience can offer and on finding the right program.

The goal of this book is not to say everything that could be said about study abroad or to convince parents that their daughter or son should study abroad, but rather to provide information useful to parents and other members of the families of students planning to study or work abroad. Some aspects of the study abroad process require more parental involvement than others. For example, parents may well become quite involved in selecting and applying to a program, arranging financial aid, working out budgets, and planning transportation. They may become less involved in obtaining necessary academic approvals, selecting courses, making overseas housing arrangements, and planning side trips. More than anything, they provide on-going emotional support for what may be the primary adventure in their daughter's or son's young adulthood.

The term "study abroad" is used here to describe what U.S. students can learn via participation in a broad spectrum of formal overseas educational programs, including work and volunteer programs. Tourism—students traveling independently, or, as students might put it, just hanging out in other countries—is not the subject of this publication.

The motivation of your daughter or son to leave the campus for a portion of her or his degree studies is seldom the result of one factor alone. Campuses themselves often send a variety of messages to students about the value of study abroad. Peer pressure and institutional rhetoric and precedent are often major forces in a student's decision. On campuses where a large proportion of students study abroad—between a quarter and a half at private, liberal arts institutions these days—students either enter with a strong incentive to do so or learn very quickly that this is something they should seriously consider. On campuses where study abroad is very much a marginal activity—for example, at many large public universities, where only about 2 to 5 percent study abroad—the motivation to do so might have to come from other sources.

The parental role in helping make the decision is likely to be something already begun. This has to do with the complex of signals and messages about internationalism and seeking out new ways of living and learning which parents inevitably (and often unconsciously) have communicated to their family over the years. Ample evidence exists to show that children of parents who have traveled, worked, or studied abroad are much more likely themselves to seek out this experience, and to be supported in this decision. It can also be the case that this role model influence can work negatively, so that parents who have not themselves had an international experience can convey, often without intending to do so, that it is not so important. There is also the chance, young adulthood being what it is, that students will rebel against whatever their parents have or have not done, in an attempt to assert their own independence.

Choosing whether or not to study abroad must be a personal decision on the part of your daughter or son. Too much parental pressure one way or the other can interfere with the essential thinking-through which each student must do, largely on her or his own. Students who are cajoled or forced into study abroad by external pressures—not just parents, but also friends, individual faculty, academic and study abroad advisers, academic policies, or other more general social influences—often have trouble adjusting to its many challenges. Those who are dissuaded from studying abroad by one or more of these same pressures sometimes later resent this, regretting that they did not follow their own impulses—especially when their friends who did study abroad return to the campus saying it was the best thing they ever did. The key is to let your daughter or son know that you are open to discussing the many alternatives that exist.

Study abroad at its best combines academic and experiential learning, but the combination of these educational modes differs from program to program. On the conservative, academic extreme, there are credit-bearing, classroom-centered programs that take place on foreign soil. On the liberal, experiential extreme, there is practical, hands-on, field work: unpaid internships, paid short-term work, volunteer projects, teaching, and independent study undertaken in an overseas work-place or social setting, often with no expectation of receiving U.S. degree credit. Between these poles exists a variety of hybrid learning models, each with a different mix of academic and experiential structures.

Campus study abroad advisers are ideally positioned to provide the most informed and professional counsel for your daughter or son. Admittedly, they are proactive supporters of the experience of studying abroad, or they would not be in their current position. But they are also able to provide disinterested advice for students who are exploring the pros and cons of studying abroad. They do this with the experience of having advised many other students not perhaps dissimilar to your daughter or son, and having worked with these students before, during, and after the overseas sojourn.

They know that study abroad is not for every student. Advisers understand the importance of furnishing students with the best information and guidance, then letting them make up their own minds. Advisers are of course pleased to have opportunities to talk with parents, but they see their primary role as that of working with students. Advisers are uniquely positioned to help with the complex of institutional considerations, such as credit approval and financial aid.

Part 1 of the book presents the four main arguments in support of study abroad: that it enriches and diversifies curricular opportunities, deepens cross-cultural understanding, enhances career prospects, and builds intellectual maturity and self-confidence. For readers interested in the history and development of study abroad as an essential dimension of U.S. higher education, there is a short chapter on this topic. Part 3 provides an overview of the many considerations that that go into selecting the right program. Part 4 covers the myriad things that must be done before departure by students and parents alike. Part 5 conveys to parents a sense of what the overseas living and learning experience is like for students. The final section suggests the various ways students will react to their overseas experience once it ends and offers strategies they can use to adapt that experience to their studies and life.

A Note on Student Privacy

Policies on protecting students' privacy vary from institution to institution. Some colleges, for example, do not forward grade reports to parents' addresses, believing that they belong to the student. Parents who do not understand or agree with the privacy policy of their offspring's institution sometimes become frustrated when representatives of the institution decline to release information about the student (concerning illness, legal problems, or a change of address, for example) unless the student authorizes the release. At points in the book, we urge parents to contact the study abroad office for information. Parents should keep in mind that study abroad advisers are usually glad to provide whatever information they can, but that in some cases they may be bound by institutional policy not to release certain information without the explicit permission of the student.

Acknowledgments

This book could not have been written without the collective knowledge, seasoned perspective, and warm friendship shared over the years with my professional colleagues in NAFSA's Section on U.S. Students Abroad, known as SECUSSA.

An only slightly-less-general debt of gratitude is owed to the many contributors to NAFSA's *Guide to Education Abroad for Advisers and Administrators,* and to my coeditors on that volume, John Pearson and Marvin Slind. In particular, I wish to acknowledge my thanks to the following individuals for material I have adapted from *Education Abroad*: Bill Nolting, University of Michigan; Clay Hubbs, Hampshire College; Mary Anne Grant, International Student Exchange Program; Maria Krane, Nebraska Wesleyan University; Heidi Soneson, Richard Warzecha, and Margaret Warpeha, University of Minnesota; Cheryl Lochner-Wright, University of Wisconsin-Eau Claire; Joseph Navari, Linfield College; Joan Raducha, University of Wisconson-Madison; Michael Monahan, Macalester College; Larry Laffrey, Ball State University; Kathkeen Sideli, Indiana University; Stephen Cooper, Louisiana State University; Nancy Stubbs, University of Colorado; Jane Cary, Princeton University; Rosalind Hoffa, Amherst College; Mickey Hanzel Slind, ISA/Butler University; Deborah Herrin, Optical Society of America; William Cressey, CIEE; Susan Brick, Whitman College; Ellen Summerfield, Linfield College; Rebecca Sibley, University of Colorado; Helen Stellmacher, St. Olaf College; and John Henderson, Dickinson College.

Some portions of the text represent reworkings of writing I have published elsewhere. A version of the brief history of study abroad appeared in the introductory section of *Peterson's Guide* (1995). The section on how potential employers assess the experience of study abroad appeared in several issues of *Transitions Abroad* magazine. Some of the pragmatic counsel on preparing for study abroad and on culture shock appeared in student handbooks I wrote for Brown University, Pomona College, and studyabroad.com. Some of the discussion of the emerging global culture appeared in NAFSA's *International Educator* magazine.

Special thanks go to Susan Brick, Whitman College; John Henderson, Dickinson College; and John Pearson, Stanford University, for reading a completed draft of the manuscript and making suggestions for improving its content and usefulness. Thanks, also, to Kirstin Moritz, Brown University; Harlan Henson,

Auburn University; David Fenner, University of Washington; and JoAnn Wallace, Antioch College, who, with Susan Brick furnished quotes from students on their study abroad experience.

All data used in this book come from the Institute of International Education's annual survey of international education activity to and from U.S. colleges and universities.

I also want to thank the SECUSSA national team for its backing of this publication, and Steven Kennedy, NAFSA's Director of Publications for the original impetus, financial support during the writing period, terrific editing, and supportive collegiality throughout the birthing process.

Finally, without the love, friendship, and understanding of my wife, Rosalind, I would not have been able to undertake, much less complete, this writing.

William W. Hoffa
Amherst, Massachusetts
February 1998

□ □ □

Part 1

The Case for Study Abroad

My expectations changed a lot during the course of my time abroad. I originally embarked as an escape process. I needed to get away, do some thinking, and maybe redefine who I thought I was and what I was doing. As the semester progressed I started to pay more attention to the economy, landscape, and politics of Spain. Then my focus changed again from getting to know Spain to getting to know my own country. By living in a different environment I was given a different glimpse of life in the United States. That made me think about the world and its future and my place in it. I think it doesn't really matter why you begin a foreign study adventure, because for as many reasons as you think of, many more will pop up during the experience. It is important to have a focus, but also to recognize that the focus may change and that that change indicates you are getting the full benefit from your experience. —CHRISTINA WARD, SPAIN

In a world becoming every year more interdependent, the educational value to students of spending at least some portion of their undergraduate years living and learning in another country is no longer really debatable. The global competence and alertness students gain through such an experience is crucial to American national interests, as well as to the interests of students themselves. Today, students who leave college without having had a significant globalizing experience as part of their undergraduate education may appear to employers as not fully educated for the world they are entering.

Study abroad encourages self-reflection. Seeing ourselves as others see us— and ultimately, perhaps, as we are—is something not easy to do at home. Put another way, fish never know they are wet, because they lack the contrast of air. As anthropologists tell us, we travel with our cultural baggage. That baggage simultaneously identifies us to others and filters out that which we are unwilling or unable to see and know. Learning comes through the gradual process of shedding as much baggage as possible and seeing anew.

As students learn about the foreignness of other lands, cultures, and people, they learn invaluable lessons about themselves as Americans. Perhaps for the first time, they become able to distinguish those parts of themselves that are products of their time and place in American society from those that are universal. This degree of personal and national self-knowledge cannot be gained at home, whatever the resources of their college or university and however high their personal motivation.

Isolationism and Internationalism: Poles of the American Experience

The role of the United States as a leader among nations is changing rapidly. Despite our position of international leadership for almost fifty years, we are ill-prepared for the changes in business, manufacturing, diplomacy, science and technology that have come with an intensely interdependent world. Effectiveness in such a world requires a citizenry whose knowledge is sufficiently international in scope to cope with global interdependence.

—ADVISORY COUNCIL FOR INTERNATIONAL EDUCATIONAL EXCHANGE, EDUCATING FOR GLOBAL COMPETENCE, 1988

Despite of our heritage as a nation of immigrants, our geography has, for most of our national history, kept us at home and other lands at a distance. Beginning with George Washington, we have heard from our national leaders about the dangers of involving ourselves too much in the affairs of other countries and losing our native integrity and self-sufficiency.

At its best, study abroad:

■ Enriches and diversifies undergraduate education by offering courses, programs, and academic learning of a sort not available on the home campus

■ Provides U.S. students with a global outlook that emphasizes the ties among nations and cultures, the universality of human values, and the necessity of working together

■ Enhances career preparation by teaching cross-cultural and workplace skills of value to today's employers, often through internships and other hands-on experiences

■ Deepens intellectual and personal maturity, fosters independent thinking, and builds self-confidence.

As a nation we have ventured abroad in significant numbers only when provoked by dramatic external threats to our domestic security or "the American way of life." The most notable examples of those overseas ventures fall within the memory of parents of today's students: our joining with the Allies to defeat the totalitarianism of Nazi Germany in World War II, and our opposition to the spread of communism during the Cold War.

Isolationist thinking has also often fostered the illusion of national self-dependency, of being separate in our national destiny from the rest of the world and the feeling that other nations and cultures have little or nothing to teach us. Even our full participation in international bodies such as the United Nations is frequently constrained by the fear that American sovereignty will be sacrificed in favor of a "one-world" illusion of internationalism.

There is, of course, an equally strong internationalist strain to American culture. We have always been a nation of imports and exports, and we have been diplomatically active throughout our history. The international dimension of American culture is celebrated in our long heritage of making room in the national fold for successive waves of immigrants from all corners of the world. This is what Walt Whitman celebrated when he called America, "a Nation of nations." Our awareness of this heterogeneous diversity at home promotes the illusion, however, that we are more international than our perspectives and actions reveal us to be.

Another limiting factor in U.S. thinking about the rest of the world has been the emergence over the last half-century of English as the world language. This linguistic and cultural development has unfortunately had the effect of allowing Americans to think that any accommodations that need to be made with the rest of the world can or will be made on our linguistic and cultural terms.

Today English is indeed likely to be spoken by the majority of educated world travelers and other "world citizens." It is also spoken by businessmen who are successfully selling their products on our shores, and by just about anyone involved in international tourism. But English is not the language spoken by most people in most countries as a native language, something any seasoned traveler can confirm. Among those who know it, it is spoken in addition to the language they speak at home, and perhaps other languages they have also learned.

> *The world in which most adult Americans grew to maturity no longer exists. The cold war is over. The domestic economy is global. The "melting pot" is boiling over. Our world is in flux. . . . Unless today's students develop the competence to function effectively in a global environment, they are unlikely to succeed in the 21st century.*

> —AMERICAN COUNCIL ON EDUCATION,
> EDUCATING AMERICANS FOR A WORLD IN FLUX, 1995

The "out of sight, out of mind" approach toward other lands and other cultures is now not only unrealistic, but also clearly detrimental. Our nation is involved in world affairs as never before, and our long-range economic and social well-being stems from this successful involvement. Like it or not, our national economic and social destiny can seldom be separated completely from what is happening in other corners of the globe.

It is thus vital that we learn to see ourselves as others see us. This is not because foreign perceptions are necessarily right—indeed, Americans and their country are often woefully misunderstood elsewhere, in part because of the misleading images we export. Nevertheless, our progress as a nation depends on clear-sightedness and pragmatism about ourselves and about the vast majority of the planet that may be dramatically different from what we imagine it to be.

In view of the expanding web of cultural and economic ties in which we are all enmeshed, it is surprising that, numerically at least, study abroad remains a marginal activity in U.S. higher education. The estimated 100,000 students who study or work abroad in a given academic year constitute less than 1 percent of the more than 14 million students enrolled in U.S. higher education. Those unfamiliar with its many educational and career benefits still characterize study abroad as something essential only for foreign language majors. For others it is seen as an escape from domestic academic pressures; an elitist activity for the affluent few with money to burn; an extra, a diversion, a tangent, something for dilettantes, but not for serious students; or as a bonus or privilege for the academically superior.

> *The Nation must commit itself now to providing all students with the kinds of knowledge it once provided to only a few—a powerful, deep-rooted understanding of other languages, diverse cultures, and global issues.*
>
> —AMERICAN COUNCIL ON EDUCATION,
> EDUCATING AMERICANS FOR A WORLD IN FLUX, 1995

These anachronistic and misleading characterizations of study abroad usually stem from unfamiliarity or ignorance and tend to be heard most often on campuses with little or no study abroad activity. To the extent they are propagated by university faculty and administrators, they may disguise institutional fears and problems. Some administrators at private, fee-driven institutions are concerned about the effect of study abroad on institutional budgets as students' tuition payments are rerouted into study abroad programs. Faculty, for their part, often do not want their best students, especially those majoring in their discipline, to disappear during the year. Residence life administrators worry about empty beds, admissions offices about finding well-qualified transfer students, and financial aid offices about having to recalculate financial aid packages.

On the other hand, admissions offices report that questions about study abroad opportunities are among the top three asked by high school students trying to decide on colleges, while at many private institutions the proportion of students who study abroad at some point during their undergraduate years can

Trends in Study Abroad

Currently, almost 90,000 students receive academic credit from U.S. institutions for study abroad. This number represents a near doubling from the 1985–86 figure of 48,500.

About two-thirds of all U.S. students study in Europe; 15 percent in Latin America; 6 percent in Asia; and less than 3 percent in each of the other regions of the world. The United Kingdom accounts for about a quarter of all enrollments. The other top host countries are France, Spain, Italy, Germany, Japan, Israel, Costa Rica, Australia, and Russia. The percentage of students studying in Europe has dropped slowly, as enrollments in Latin America have risen.

Almost three-quarters of all students studying abroad do so in a program sponsored by or affiliated with their home institution; the remainder choose programs sponsored by other institutions.

About half of all study abroaders are juniors; 16 percent are seniors; 12 percent are sophomores; and the remainder are recent graduates. Their majors are humanities and social sciences (35 percent); business (14 percent); languages (11 percent) ; fine arts (7 percent); and physical sciences (7 percent); with smaller percentages from other majors. As the overseas curriculum for study abroad expands, more students from academic fields not traditionally represented in study abroad will begin to show up in the figures.

Almost two-thirds of study abroaders are women, a long-standing disproportion that is slowly beginning to even out as the overseas curriculum broadens to include fields such as business, science, engineering, and other traditionally male areas of concentration.

Only about 12-13 percent of study abroaders go overseas for an entire academic year. Another 39 percent do so for a semester, with the remainder going abroad for less than a semester. Year-long programs have declined steadily as a percentage of all study abroad, while the popularity of short-term programs continues to grow. In contrast, throughout the early decades of study abroad full academic year programs predominated.

The percentage of white students who study abroad (84 percent) exceeds their overall representation in U.S. higher education (72 percent), but the socioeconomic and racial diversity of study abroad students is gradually increasing. Cost is the primary barrier. At private institutions where all financial aid can be applied to overseas studies, participation in study abroad programs by students from minority backgrounds is equal to that of white students.

be as high as 30 to 50 percent of each graduating class. Clearly, many students find living and learning overseas of great interest and importance.

Enriching and Diversifying Home Campus Studies

Study abroad provides a wonderful opportunity to augment the curriculum available to your son or daughter here at home. Consider the appeal of studying marine biology in the West Indies, acting in London, art history in Florence, or development issues in Latin America, South Asia, or Africa. In most cases, with careful planning, students can get full academic credit for their overseas studies.

Depending on the campus, student, and program, credit can be earned in one or more academic categories:

- In the academic major or minor

- To satisfy general education or broad degree requirements

- To fulfill elective requirements

- As residential or transfer credit.

During the years when the "junior year abroad" was the most common form of study abroad, it served the curricular needs and interests primarily of students majoring in language and cultural studies. Given the strong western European emphasis of many U.S. colleges and universities, especially with regard to the languages then taught, most junior year abroad students found themselves in France, Italy, Germany, or Spain. Students without proficiency in a foreign language studied in Britain or Ireland. Almost all JYA students were drawn from the humanities or social sciences.

This traditional bias has over time given way to an enlarged view of study abroad as something that can be done across the curriculum. That is, there are very few academic fields for which at least some overseas course work, offered in one or more programs, is not now available. The best overview of the tremendous variety and range of current curricular offerings is seen in the annual guides to study abroad programming, IIE's *Academic Year Abroad* and *Vacation Study Abroad,* and Peterson's *Study Abroad.* A brief summation demonstrates the richness of available options.

LANGUAGE LEARNING

Students whose primary interest is in the acquisition of a western Europe language can now choose from the huge variety of traditional language and cultural immersion programs. U.S. language department faculty, founders of most of the programs available to students, continue to believe that there is no better way to gain language proficiency than by living and learning in the place where the language is spoken.

In addition, a veritable host of less commonly taught languages can be pursued through study abroad programs. The list is long: Arabic, Czech, Chinese, Danish, Dutch, Finnish, Gaelic, Ancient Greek, Modern Greek, Hausa, Hebrew, Hindi, Hungarian, Indonesian, Japanese, Korean, Latvian, Nepali, Norwegian, Polish, Portuguese, Russian, Shona, Swahili, Swedish, Tamil, Telugu, Thai, Tibetan Twa, Turkish, Turkmen, Ukrainian, Vietnamese, Welsh, Xhosa, Yiddish, Yoruba, Zulu. Many of these languages are not taught on U.S. campuses, even at major universities—Japanese, Chinese, Russian are the exceptions—and so studying one of them overseas may be the only way to gain exposure or deepen proficiency.

Students in cultural immersion and area-studies programs study the local language to learn at least its rudiments. Making an attempt to learn the language of one's hosts is always appreciated, especially by host families. Even students who do not achieve full proficiency learn far more in native settings than they ever could at home.

COURSE WORK IN THE MAJOR (IN ENGLISH)

Four contemporary factors make it possible for U.S. students to do serious academic course work overseas largely in English. These are:

■ The development of short-term, summer, quarter, semester, and academic-year programs set up and operated in English by U.S. colleges and universities overseas

■ The existence of special English-language programs in non-English-speaking countries, set up for foreigners (sometimes specifically for Americans, sometimes not) by overseas institutions

■ The growing number of universities in countries where English is widely spoken—such as the Netherlands, Bulgaria, Hong Kong, Denmark, Sweden, Norway, and Finland—which offer a partial or full curriculum in English for their own students and now welcome students from other countries

■ The increasing willingness of universities and other institutions in English-speaking countries to allow the short-term matriculation of overseas students—especially in the United Kingdom, Ireland, Australia, New Zealand, and now South Africa.

Although it is tempting to lament our national monolingualism, the other side of the coin is the incredible array of study abroad opportunities that would not otherwise be available to your daughter or son.

AREA AND CULTURAL STUDIES

Most U.S. colleges and universities offer one or more area studies majors or programs at the undergraduate level, which also may exist as a minor. Latin American Studies, Asian Studies, and European Studies are perhaps the most common. Such concentrations draw upon course work offered in several academic departments.

Study abroad programs designed to complement area studies programs enable students to experience, in their daily living and learning, the culture they are studying. Obviously there can be no U.S.-based substitute for this unique opportunity. Being surrounded by the artifacts and monuments of history, seeing where and how people live, and learning their language and customs allows students to get under the skin of the culture and at times to feel part of it.

Beyond the study abroad programs that supplement typical area studies offerings, many programs focus on regions and cultures not well represented in the home-campus curriculum. Some focus on the cultural, economic, or political unity of a broad region, for example, the Middle East, South Asia, or Oceania.

Other area studies programs have a narrower focus, stressing the historical unity of a national culture within the area under study. These are taught in English, with language study as an option.

A smaller number of area studies programs delve into some of the historical cultures that now exist as subcultures within one or more large nation states. Thus, there are programs focusing on the Aboriginal culture that survives in Australia, Brazil, and Canada; the sea-linked cultures of the Caribbean and Mediterranean; the ancient Amazonian culture of Brazil and Ecuador; the Celtic and Gaelic heritage of contemporary Ireland and Scotland; Hebraic culture as it exists in Israel and wherever Jews have lived across Europe, Africa, and North America; the Maori culture of New Zealand; Mayan culture in Mexico; the defiant Basque culture in Spain; and even Classical and Renaissance civilization as it has affected Greece, England, and Italy.

With the right preparation, good courses, linked excursions, and meaningful contacts with local people, students find their interest and motivation to learn boosted greatly. More often than not they come away saying how much they have learned in such a short period.

INTERDISCIPLINARY AND GLOBAL STUDIES

Few subjects can be fully understood within the confines of one academic discipline; few lack an international dimension. But certain fields are by definition more interdisciplinary and more global than others. These involve issues and questions that transcend national borders and cultural confines. Understanding global systems often means focusing studies on problems, rather than on geographical regions or academic disciplines. Common examples of such problem-centered academic programs include: American Studies, African-American Studies, Ecology/Environmental Studies, Health Studies, Conservation Studies, Ethnic Studies, Communications, International Relations, Urban Studies, Women's Studies, and so on. Student interest in any of these areas can be pursued through participation in a study abroad program.

Learning about Culture and National Identity through Study Abroad

The traditional rationale for study abroad was that it provided the opportunity for students to assimilate another culture. That rationale still holds for the 12-13 percent of study abroad students who spend an entire academic year abroad and thus have time for a thorough bicultural experience. What about the 88 percent of students who spend a shorter period abroad? What do they learn about culture? One answer is related to the emergence, for better or worse, of the first-ever global culture.

No matter how much time is spent abroad, your daughter or son will find that the new global culture is permeating and challenging all other cultures, including our own. It is hard to overestimate the impact of ubiquitous and pervasive presences such as:

■ Multinational commercial corporations—including not only technological giants such as Sony, GM, and Microsoft, but also popular culture food purveyors like McDonalds, clothing manufacturers and distributors like Nike, and hotel chains like Marriott and Holiday Inn

■ Global computer and satellite communications companies like CNN

■ Global distribution networks for industrial products and services, and for popular culture (movies, television, clothing and fashion, music)

■ Global securities markets and banking systems that allow the rapid movement of money and credit across borders

■ Global outsourcing, tariff-free trade agreements, and visa-free and even passport-free borders.

The political, economic, and technological realities that support the worldwide mobility of people, capital, and ideas are building the new global culture at home and abroad. Seeing its power and influence outside our national boundaries is for U.S. students usually very eye-opening. They grow to understand how much of the global culture is driven by U.S. power and influence. Even more surprising to our students is how much is not, and how many other countries are powerful players in the new world system. Finally, they learn that much global activity has no single national base; that ownership, materials, labor, and distribution are truly international.

Worldwide multicultural and multiethnic realities now either strongly influence or dominate the social reality of almost all developed and developing countries. For that reason, finding global commonalities while learning to value and respect cultural differences has become an essential component of U.S. degree studies. Living and learning overseas is for students an important preparation for the social and multicultural realities that dominate the emerging multicultural work and living environment—in Boston and Bangkok, Singapore and Seattle, and any other global village that one calls home.

A by-product of such insights is quite often a new and positive awareness of the many positive aspects of American life. While all students learn that other cultures and countries have their own character and appeal, they also return with a refreshed appreciation of the United States. Many come back praising our cultural diversity, openness, natural space and beauty, efficiency, economic vitality, and optimistic spirit. Almost all gain a new respect for the American academic system, and for their own college or university in particular.

Thus, while your son or daughter may or may not "acquire" the traditional host culture of the study abroad destination, it is likely that he or she will experience something even more significant: a wake-up call to a complex sense of contemporary cultural heterogeneity, to the emerging global culture, to a new synergy between things here and there, to his or her own American identity and to our national presence and power in a changing world environment.

Deepening Personal Identity, Maturity, Independence, and Confidence

Study abroad can be for students a personally transforming experience, a quantum leap in their intellectual and social development. No two students are likely to have quite the same experience or to respond in the same way to that experience, regardless of their plans, motivations, and circumstances.

It is almost guaranteed that your son or daughter will say that studying abroad was one of the best things he or she ever did. Students praise the overseas living and learning experience as having had a major impact on how they feel and think about themselves, about their national identity as Americans, and about the world. They will talk with pride about all the personal and intercultural obstacles they learned to overcome, about the hard times and the many joyful moments. Many will express a yearning to go back as soon as possible, and most will recommend the experience to other students and parents. Most stare with wonder over what they would have missed had they not had the courage and good sense to do it.

In discussing the total educational value of their time abroad, students will invariably stress opportunities they had to challenge, test, and get to know themselves. They will comment on what it was like, often for the first time in their lives, to be truly away from home, away from friends and family, familiar habits and surroundings. They will talk about the experience of going through culture shock (discussed in Part 5), of being an outsider in an environment whose rules and cues they did not understand initially. Many describe it as the hardest thing they ever did, but, because of it, say that they returned more tolerant, confident, and mature because they were able to test themselves against this adversity.

When taking an excursion to see a monument commemorating a battle being discussed in class or touring a farm growing grapes used to make local wine, new connections are made. Meeting a worker on a train who tells them how it "really is" in the country and what will happen in the next election, or talking with a soldier back from service with the United Nations in Bosnia, and other such encounters with native people offer insights and nuances of meaning not found in textbooks. Processing this new information is something students realize they must do for themselves, and they do. The new cognitive skills they develop abroad affect the way they go about learning when they return to their home campus.

Improving Career Prospects in the Global Economy

Technological developments and innovations, once largely the province of the United States and other industrialized western economies, now come from nearly all countries. India and Ireland are leading purveyors of computer software. Southeast Asia leads the world in textile design and modern production techniques. Finland has the best engineering for high-tech dental equipment and cellular telephones. Sweden is as advanced as any nation in the use of industrial robots. U.S. quality control in automobile and other sorts of manufacturing became competitive with Japan's only after we copied Japan's methods and slowly caught up.

The winds of internationalism, in short, now reach all corners of the earth. Today's students are challenged to ride these winds and chart courses that take advantage of their prevailing directions. Most local and national economies, hitherto thought to be partially or exclusively self-sufficient, are linked to a powerful and vast array of international forces and influences. It is in fact hard not to be involved in the global marketplace, wherever one works, whatever one does.

Raw materials for products sold locally and internationally, for instance, seldom originate in the same places where manufacturing and trade take place. They need to be imported or exported, often from and to the corners of the earth. In turn, manufactured goods are increasingly designed to be sold in countries beyond their origin. In the growing service industry, new concepts, technologies, and other essential information and ideas are seldom the exclusive property of one nation. Instead, they cross borders in the contemporary world even faster than people and goods do. Whatever their origin, they are applied worldwide.

This interdependence of all parts of the working world means that those who can bring to their domestic responsibilities a heightened degree of international awareness are more likely to be hired—and then to succeed. Employers increasingly recognize that applicants who have studied, worked, or even traveled extensively abroad are likely to possess the personal qualities demanded by this new environment:

- Personal maturity
- The courage to take risks
- Imagination
- Adaptability
- Grit
- Self-confidence
- An awareness that the rest of the world does not always operate according to U.S. standards and terms, or in English.

Study abroad, on its own, unsupported by substantive professional or technical knowledge and work experience, typically does not qualify college seniors for the international career that so many come back from overseas imagining: holding a managerial position in an overseas setting with a multinational enterprise that operates simultaneously in many countries, making, buying, and selling products and services around the world.

But it can help graduates focus their career search and even give them an edge when seeking the increasing number of jobs that have an international component. Variants of the "internationalized career" require routine overseas communications in English or a foreign language and regular short-term trips abroad to conduct business, do market research, or offer consultations. Other sorts of domestic work provide opportunities for short-term postings abroad, for example, to oversee the expansion of new operations or the installation of new technologies. Such home-based, but still internationalized careers exist not only in commerce, banking, law, communications, engineering, and science, but also in the nonprofit service sector, in government, higher education and scholarship, and volunteer service organizations.

Any study and work abroad can also be seen as a practical experience, an investment in the future, almost regardless of duration or destination. Engineers and scientists, businessmen and economic developers, social workers and environmentalists, all increasingly understand that what graduates need to compete successfully in the global marketplace is not only technical knowledge and skills, but also a global perspective and the ability to perform in a cross-cultural context. Foreign exposure builds those personal capacities that most employers are seeking. The experience of being abroad has a tendency to focus student attention on what comes next. Not infrequently, students return expressing an immediate interest in "going back" as soon as possible. Sometimes this translates into thoughts of returning after graduation to live and work, sometimes into a more open-ended decision to seek an international career.

Conclusion

In sum, there are many reasons why study abroad can matter tremendously in the education of your daughter or son, though some may carry more weight than others in the thinking of any individual or family. It is important to consider all of them in making the decision whether to pursue this experience. If the decision is positive, the next challenge is to choose the programs that represent the best fit, the ones that will maximize the possibility of achieving personal, educational, and career-preparation goals. This involves knowing how programs differ from each other, then weighing these variables against each other and coming up with one or more optimal choices.

□   □   □

Part 2

Study Abroad in U.S. Higher Education: A Brief Historical Tour

The idea of traveling to other countries for part of one's higher education is nothing new. Medieval monks and Renaissance scholars such as Erasmus sought wisdom throughout Europe, often traveling far and wide in search of libraries and other scholars from whom they could learn. What is different in today's world is that such travel has evolved from being more or less a luxury for the privileged and academic few to a necessity for students seeking to become globally competent and fully prepared for the challenges of the new century.

From America's earliest days, wealthy colonists sent their sons to European universities to compensate for the perceived weaknesses of American institutions. John Quincy Adams, son of President John Adams, to cite one example, acquired his formal education at the Passy Academy outside Paris. The elitist pattern of study abroad continued through the end of nineteenth century, when a European grand tour or postgraduate study at a German or British university was seen as an essential component of a well-rounded gentleman's education. Study abroad was for those few who could afford it, understood its value, and were preparing themselves for leadership roles.

Often such young scholars merely wandered, guided by whim and opportunity. Sometimes they sought out world-famous mentors, becoming their disciples and apprentices. Occasionally they actually matriculated in venerable foreign universities, although few took examinations or sought degrees. Future American scientists, engineers, architects, physicians, businessmen, lawyers, politicians, artists, writers, and of course scholars traveled overseas to see what the Old World had to offer the New. So did future presidents, such as Teddy Roosevelt, who studied German and French in Dresden in 1873.

In the early decades of the twentieth century, as American higher education, especially at the graduate and professional school levels, was beginning to operate on world standards, a previously powerful rationale for overseas study diminished. Nevertheless, something of the allure of foreign study persists to this day, an allure embodied in highly competitive and prestigious postgraduate awards such as the Rhodes, Marshall, and Fulbright fellowships. Bill Clinton, awarded a postgraduate Rhodes Scholarship to study at Oxford University, was the fourth U.S. president to study abroad.

These early forms of study abroad were, as might be expected, largely male endeavors. Male careers took precedence in most families and within most institutions. Some well-to-do female students, on the other hand, also traveled overseas for broad educational purposes during the same time period, typically to acquire European manners, refinement, or even a husband—as dramatized in the fiction of Henry James and Edith Wharton. Indeed, gender demarcations of the time steered women toward "culture" and marriage, whereas men were expected to pursue riches and fame in the world. Women sojourners being introduced to the arts, history, and refinements of Europe traveled with their families, maiden aunts, or in small groups with tutors. Few enrolled in European universities, but many were able to pursue educational goals not equally available at home.

Study abroad as we know it today was not an institutionalized part of American higher education until just after World War I. The first twentieth-century model, beginning in the 1920s, came to be known as junior year abroad. JYA began when several mainly private, mainly eastern women's colleges—Sweetbriar, Smith, Marymount, plus the University of Delaware—set up year-long programs in Europe for their junior language majors. In so doing, they transformed the enlightening but informal educational tour of earlier times into a creditable academic experience, part of degree studies. JYA was based on the assumption that language and cultural studies could best be pursued in an overseas setting that fully immersed students in the daily life of a foreign land. The number of JYA programs grew slowly over the two decades between the wars. World War II forced the suspension of all such programs.

During the 1940s and 1950s, as part of postwar reconciliation efforts on both sides of the Atlantic, a slow expansion of educational programs and exchanges took place on many American campuses. Most prewar programs resumed, and additional colleges began to offer similar opportunities for their students. Among these were Middlebury, Fordham, Sarah Lawrence, Georgetown, Lake Erie College, Oberlin, Tulane and Sophie Newcomb, Antioch, and Stanford.

When the war receded further, the U.S government began to support programs and initiatives to send teachers and scholars to other parts of the world to lecture and do research. Foremost among these were the Fulbright program, begun in 1946, the Agency for International Development, and the language and area studies programs funded under Title VI of the Higher Education Act. In the late 1950s, the National Defense Education Act, a product of Cold War anxiety about Soviet achievements in science and technology, supported language learning on U.S. campuses and abroad.

   As the reconstruction of Europe proceeded under the Marshall Plan, other nations began to send their students to the United States in ever-growing numbers in recognition of America's new power and authority in the world. Large public universities initiated institution-to-institution exchange activities, sometimes with U.S. government support. Thus American students (chiefly graduate students) and students from foreign universities took each others' places as part of reciprocal international agreements, supplementing the earlier JYA program model. University-to-university exchanges of students and scholars continue to be a major component of the U.S. study abroad picture.
   During the 1950s and 1960s, faculty and graduate students who had spent time abroad returned to their campuses inspired to set up overseas experiences for their students. In some cases U.S. students matriculated directly into foreign universities; in other instances, they studied in what amounted to overseas branch campuses. It was during these decades that the idea of study abroad as a means of bolstering and broadening undergraduate education began to become firmly established. With this acceptance came needed campus support services and more formalized student advising for both incoming and outgoing students. NAFSA, founded in 1948 as the National Association of Foreign Student Advisers, added its Section on U.S. Students Abroad in 1970.
   Throughout the 1960s and into the late 1970s many U.S. institutions, especially large public and private universities, set up new programs exclusively for their own students. Among these were Syracuse, the University of California and California State University systems, the city and state university systems of New York, Dartmouth, Indiana, Penn State, Brigham Young, New York University, Rutgers, and the University of Colorado. Some private colleges (for example, Kalamazoo, Beloit, and Goshen) thought living and learning abroad were so essential that they created opportunities for virtually all students to study abroad. By 1970, study abroad programs were an accepted feature of an undergraduate education, affecting an estimated 20,000 students each year. With inexpensive air travel, youth hostels, and a strong U.S. dollar, many more students began to travel abroad to see the sights. Such pleasure trips often became the inspiration for returning to study or work.
   Some American students had participated in European work programs and reconstruction projects in the years immediately following WWII. Others, from religious backgrounds, did missionary work all over the world. But the idea of going abroad to gain invaluable international experience and perhaps to give something back to the world was deepened by the social and political ferment of the 1960s. President Kennedy—who had himself studied at the London School of Economics during the summer of 1935—founded the Peace Corps in 1961.
   The Peace Corps was the most prominent of volunteer service opportunities, but it was far from being the only program of its sort. Many other volunteer and service-learning programs, such as Operation Crossroads Africa and

the Partnership for Service Learning, also provided exciting new chances for college graduates to express their idealism and gain practical experience living on the terms of a foreign culture. Their tremendous appeal, which continues today, suggests not only the deeply rooted altruism of American students and their desire to make a difference in the world, but also the fact that experiential education abroad was an idea which had gained wide acceptance within the context of American higher education.

From the end of the Vietnam war in 1975 to the fall of the Berlin Wall and the collapse of world communism in the early 1990s, the international situation was often tense and unsettled. As the U.S. economy rose and fell and American industry lost many of its world markets, the need to come to grips with global politics and trade became evident to more educational institutions and students. Thus, in spite of the isolationist aftermath of the U.S. involvement in Vietnam, successive oil crises, the rise of international terrorism, and the decline of the U.S dollar, a growing number of American undergraduates felt the need to take a first-hand look at the world through participation in an academic program or work experience abroad.

In world terms, U.S. educational institutions have been almost alone in sponsoring study abroad as an option within the undergraduate degree. Only in recent years—mainly within the European Community and in Japan—have other countries begun to follow this example. It is not that students from other countries, at all levels, do not study outside their national borders, for they do. Indeed, about 460,000 foreign students are currently studying and doing research on U.S. campuses, a number representing about a third of the world student mobility market and 3 percent of total U.S postsecondary enrollments. The difference is that the bulk of these international students are enrolled in U.S. degree programs and are thus here for as long as it takes to receive the degree. In contrast, many U.S. students attend foreign universities, but very few enroll for the purpose of earning a foreign diploma.

In sum, study abroad emanating from U.S. campuses has for three-quarters of a century been a time-honored way of enriching and diversifying U.S. undergraduate degree studies. Given the changing nature of the world, the case for study abroad has never been stronger.

□   □   □

Part 3

Selecting the Right Program

A few years ago you helped your son or daughter wrestle with the question of which college to attend. Now, in thinking about studying abroad, the question is similar. "Which program?" This time, however, the choice is being made by a young adult with several more years of independence and personal growth, someone who may be glad to have your advice but who is probably more likely to seek support for a decision she or he will make. When, where, and what to study overseas is usually something students need to think through for themselves, although there are numerous areas in which parents still play a major role.

To provide the support students need, parents should have a basic grasp of the following topics:

- How study abroad resembles and differs from domestic study

- How it is structured, and its many varieties in duration, location, and program type

- How credit is earned and used toward degree studies

- What the full costs will be

- What financial aid resources are available

- How safety can be maximized

- How the admissions process works

- Whether or not support services are available in particular locations for any special needs your son or daughter may have

- Whether or not a work abroad program would be a better choice.

All of these considerations and more must be factored into the choice of a particular study or work abroad program.

The Importance of Fit

At home, academic and experiential learning frequently coexist, but the one is seldom acknowledged as having much to do with the other. What is different overseas is that the academic and the experiential are much more clearly and closely linked, so that what happens inside and outside the classroom enrich each other in very tangible way. Study abroad students often become very aware of this synthesis.

With the assistance of parents, faculty, and study abroad advisers, students considering an international experience first need to identify the blend of academic and experiential education that will suit their learning style and personal goals. If one of those goals is earning academic credit, the choice must be acceptable to the home college or university as well. Students who need structure, guidance, discipline, and encouragement should opt for a classroom-centered program with strong on-site support staff and planned enrichment activities. Students who are already adventurous, independent, resourceful, and prepared intellectually and linguistically may choose a direct-enrollment, full-immersion program or an independent internship. Most students fall somewhere between these extremes and will be best served by programs that offer support as well as opportunities for independence.

While there is at least one right program for every student, not all programs are equally appropriate for all students. Matching students with programs is what any good campus advising system is set up to accomplish. Defining "right" in each instance depends on identifying a student's individual qualifications and optimum learning style and knowing what particular programs feature and demand.

How Study Programs Differ

First, a caveat: The choices open to your son or daughter may be limited from the start by the policies of his or her home campus. Many colleges and universities sponsor programs of their own and make it difficult for students to enroll in programs sponsored by other domestic or foreign institutions or agencies. Other colleges and universities, usually private ones, supplement their own programs with a list of preapproved programs offered by other sponsors. These are selected though institutional review and past student experience. In such cases, it is sometimes difficult or impossible to elect participation in a program not on the list.

Reasons for institutional restrictions vary from qualitative concerns about academic standards and curricular fit to practical concerns about the academic calendar, safety, and supervision. The desire to retain tuition dollars also motivates some institutions. To encourage compliance with their policies and preferences, some institutions restrict the use of financial aid provided by the institution (as opposed to federal or state aid) and make it difficult to transfer credit earned from nonapproved programs. If your daughter or son is affected by such policies, the existence of hundreds of possible programs may be largely irrelevant. It is sometimes possible, however, for students to gain an exception to such restrictions, and petition procedures for making an appeal may exist. You may well question institutional policy, but you should understand that it is usually based on compelling institutional and educational considerations.

Other institutions (more frequently public than private) have no such restrictions, but program choice may in fact still be limited in advance by cost, credit transfer policies, calendar, academic prerequisites for entry, or other factors. If the problem is one of cost alone, additional financial aid may be sought and awarded, as discussed later in this part of the guide.

Students who are able to take advantage of the superabundance of program choices should think about the ways in which study abroad programs differ. Here is a short list of considerations that will help students and their parents eliminate programs that do not meet their educational needs. Each will be discussed in detail.

- Program models
- Timing
- Duration
- Size
- Language of instruction
- Location
- Housing options
- Accommodation of special needs
- Study, work, or both?

PROGRAM MODELS

At the opposite extremes of the wide spectrum of study abroad programs are

- "Integrated programs" in which students enroll directly in a foreign educational institution for the purpose of linguistic and cultural immersion, and

- "Branch campus," "island," or "study center" programs operated by one or more U.S. universities and staffed at least in part by U.S. faculty offering U.S.-standard course work and related services.

Most programs fall between the poles but borrow selected features of each to serve institutional and student needs and expectations. Work abroad and "directed independent study" are typically individual endeavors and will not be discussed here.

Integrated Program Designs

Integrated programs range from student-initiated enrollment in a foreign institution of higher education to quid pro quo exchanges, whereby U.S. and foreign students, in accordance with institution-to-institution agreements, matriculate directly in each others' institutions. Such exchanges allow students to experience a foreign culture at first hand through participation in its educational and social system. Students build friendships with other students and host nationals and absorb the local culture. Integrated programs are likely to be cheaper than U.S. branch campus programs, but this depends on how higher education is financed in the country of destination.

Integrated programs demand students who are independent, well prepared, resourceful, adventurous, and adaptive. Students may have to make their own arrangements for travel, housing, and meals, although such matters are often handled by the host institution. When academic or personal problems arise, students may expect limited guidance from host university staff or faculty. Making friends usually takes time and effort. Finding course work that corresponds with American standards may be a problem, and the academic calendar may not correspond to that of the home campus. Much predeparture planning is essential to address such problems.

Branch Campus and Island Programs

Branch campus and island programs began as a response by U.S. colleges and universities to difficulties of coordination between U.S. and foreign systems of higher education. Such programs offer course work that fulfills home-campus degree requirements. Teaching is done fully or in part by home-campus faculty members familiar with the local culture, ensuring that U.S. standards are maintained with regard to workload, class time, grading, attendance, calendar, and the like.

Branch campuses and study centers can accommodate large numbers of students and offer plenty of curricular variety corresponding with home-campus academic specialties—as well as support services and cultural enrichment activities. While overall costs may be equivalent to the cost of study on the home campus, institutional financial aid almost always applies. For students who have never been abroad before and who need (and know they need) some guidance and direction, this more gradual and sheltered approach to living and learning in a foreign country pays great educational dividends. Most students gain confidence as time goes by and take great strides toward immersion. Even students who never venture outside the program's buffer zone at least get credit for their academic work.

Most programs try to marry the cultural and linguistic advantages of integrated programming with the pragmatic advantages and conveniences of branch campus and study center models. Some such programs offer several tracks, so that as students become more involved, venturesome, and linguistically able they can advance along more challenging paths. Sometimes courses offered by foreign institutions are supplemented by American-style course work, discussion groups, and tutorials. At their best, mixed programs offer a pragmatic and often ingenious blend of cultural enrichment of a sort not possible on the home campus.

TIMING: WHEN TO STUDY ABROAD?

Because studying abroad is so often a "productively unsettling" experience that leads students to ask and answer fundamental questions about their interests, skills, and goals, there is plenty to be said for thinking about participation earlier rather than later in the college career, usually sometime in the sophomore year (including summers).

On the other hand, the curricular strengths of study abroad programs suggest that the experience is ideally suited to juniors and seniors who have chosen an academic concentration and are seeking ways to deepen and diversify it in ways not possible on campus. Studying abroad in the senior year is not allowed by some schools, however; in others it can be done in the first semester of the senior year but not in the second.

DURATION: HOW LONG TO STUDY ABROAD?

Study abroad used to mean a commitment to a full-year of living and learning, usually a junior year abroad. This meant that students who could not be away for a full year were out of luck. Now short-term options abound, so students can find excellent program options that match the amount of time they can afford to be away from home campus studies.

A truism of campus advisers (one affirmed by returning students) is that the longer the program, the greater the intellectual and personal impact, in terms of academic benefit, cross-cultural understanding, career-preparation, and maturation. Long-term, fully integrated programs are much more likely to provide students with the cross-cultural coping skills employers seek. On the other hand, the availability of shorter programs makes study abroad a possibility for students who hitherto could not have considered it.

Long or short, the most important thing is that the program's goals be commensurate with the time allotted for their accomplishment. Parents are right to be suspicious of programs that seem to claim and promise too much, and they can play an important role in assisting their son or daughter to question such claims. Student motivation and discipline also play a big part in achieving anticipated outcomes, so these, too, should be part of the decision on how long to spend abroad.

SIZE: HOW LARGE A PROGRAM?

Group programs can vary tremendously in the number of participants. Smaller groups can be composed of as few as 5 to 10 students, whereas some programs regularly enroll 200 or more students. Smaller programs are often ideal at promoting cultural integration, but the curriculum may be quite limited and inflexible. The value of larger programs often resides in the quality, level, and range of curricular offerings, excursions, and support services. That richness, however, sometimes comes at the expense of cultural integration, as the group becomes an American ghetto.

Group size per se may be less important than two other factors: the program location (particularly whether other American programs are present in the same city and what effect this has on group dynamics and opportunities for cultural integration); and whether the program itself teaches and houses its students as opposed to having them enroll directly in a foreign university. In short, a large program that integrates its students fully or partially into a foreign university represents a quite different educational and social experience than a small program that keeps them together in the same classroom and accommodations.

LANGUAGE OF INSTRUCTION

Home campus instructors are usually the best judges of the level of foreign proficiency required to function successfully in a foreign university. The number of U.S. students who sit in foreign university classrooms alongside native students remains remarkably small, even in western Europe, although many, mostly private, institutions pride themselves in preparing their students for full linguistic immersion abroad.

Until recently, students without fluency in a foreign language were largely limited to English-speaking countries. Now, however, programs operating in English in countries where English is a second language are more and more plentiful. Some programs are set up by U.S. institutions hoping to expand study abroad participation to students who otherwise might not consider it. Others have been established by foreign universities seeking to "internationalize" the education of their own students by bringing them into contact with students from other countries, using English as the medium. U.S. students in such programs are given the opportunity to learn the native language but take other course work in English.

LOCATION

American-style study abroad began as an exclusively Eurocentric venture, and it continues to be dominated by program opportunities in Europe. But excellent program options now exist throughout the world. There remain many sound reasons for your daughter or son to choose to live and learn in a European location—especially if she or he has made language and other academic preparations for such study. In addition, new European program options now exist in eastern Europe, and in Russia and other countries formerly part of the Soviet Union.

There are also compelling arguments for considering programs in nonwestern regions. Study in a culture that is dramatically different from that of the West can be especially eye-opening and rewarding for students. Obviously, somewhat different considerations of cost, transportation, communications, ethnicity, language, safety, and health can come into play for students and parents considering programs in such locations. But well-run programs give much thought to these issues.

Study abroad programs are in many ways limited by local conditions. It is rare that a campus similar to the home campus will exist at the overseas location. In choosing a program location, students must once again focus on their principal goals for studying abroad and then investigate which locations can meet those critical goals. If your daughter's goal is to find a top-notch academic program in her major field, for example, then she should ask her study abroad adviser to help her identify locations known for excellence in that field. If she is interested in classical music, she might consider locations like Vienna that are known for their abundance of performances and world-class music teachers. If she is studying the politics or economics facing developing countries, then she should consider studying in Latin America, Africa, or South Asia, where she will see first-hand the impact of various development policies.

HOUSING OPTIONS

Where students live while overseas has a big impact on the experience they have. Make sure your son or daughter considers carefully the housing choices offered by the various programs under consideration. Typical options include living with a local host family ("homestay"), renting an apartment from a local landlord, and university residence halls. Programs that involve a lot of travel may put students in hostels or inexpensive hotel accommodations.

Students often have unrealistically high expectations for homestays. Many such situations abroad are different from their U.S. equivalents. Often host "families" may be older people who have an extra room they rent to a foreigner not because they are interested in befriending a student from the United States but to obtain supplementary income. In some locations it would be nearly impossible to find families to host U.S. students just for the experience of doing so. In major European cities, a student's relationship with his or her hosts may be close to that of a tenant and landlord.

If your son or daughter is enrolling directly in a foreign university, he or she may end up living in a university residence hall. Because major universities overseas are typically more urban and less residential than many U.S. campuses, only a very small number of local students may actually live in the residence halls. In some countries, only first-year students live in the dormitories before finding apartments in town. Because many U.S. students are in their third year, they may find they are more socially mature than the first-year students in the halls. U.S. students may be placed in dormitories intended specifically for foreign students where they will find no local students at all. Students should inquire about who lives in the halls before making their housing choice. Prior to departure, students should be clear about what the program provides in terms of bedding and furnishings.

ACCOMMODATION OF SPECIAL NEEDS

Mental health counseling, services for individuals with disabilities, accommodations for individuals with dietary restrictions, and nonsmoking eating and living arrangements are almost certain to be less prevalent at the overseas destination than they are in the United States. Students with special needs should consult with the study abroad office or the programs in which they are interested to make sure their needs can be accommodated in a given location.

In some parts of the world vegetarianism is virtually unheard of and, if students live with local residents, it might be considered rude not to eat the meat dishes prepared by the host family. Likewise, university dining halls overseas generally do not offer the wide variety of entrees available on U.S. university campuses and may offer no vegetarian options at all.

Smoking in public places, office buildings, and homes is more common in most other countries than it is in the United States. Students who cannot tolerate living in a residence hall or home where smoking is permitted should make sure a nonsmoking option is available in the programs that interest them.

STUDY, WORK, OR BOTH?

While most students going overseas participate in programs designed to fulfill their academic goals and obligations, a smaller proportion travel overseas primarily to gain practical experience, learn new skills, and increase their career prospects. Some seek programs with strong experiential dimensions and often choose to work rather than study abroad. Others go to test themselves by living in a totally different cultural environment, just for the human experience of doing so. And there are some students whose initial motivation may just be to get away, to do something different for a while, or to face the challenges of living in a different social and cultural environment. Your son or daughter probably has a complex of motivations, some conscious, others not.

About 10,000 U.S. students annually participate in noncredit overseas programs with a strong experiential emphasis. They seek out practical, hands-on, experience, believing that it will be of benefit to them after graduation—a view that career advisers and employers often encourage. What they finally do overseas may be mundane—simply finding a way of earning enough money to match expenses—except that doing so in a foreign country is usually interesting and rewarding. Many aim for preprofessional and career-related work, assuming that it will provide insights and qualifications for future employment. Just as many seek an outlet for altruistic impulses, such as volunteer or humanitarian service.

In addition to overseas academic study, international work or service experiences, as well as other forms of immersion in the daily life of a foreign culture, can contribute greatly to a student's formal academic or preprofessional education and understanding of the world, even if this educational gain is not measured in terms of academic credit.

—REPORT OF NATIONAL TASK FORCE ON UNDERGRADUATE
EDUCATION ABROAD, A NATIONAL MANDATE FOR EDUCATION ABROAD:
GETTING ON WITH THE TASK, 1990

A sizable portion of the U.S. students who find self-supporting work abroad do so via the Work Abroad program of the Council on International Educational Exchange (CIEE), although numerous other options exist—most notably, in England, through BUNAC. Under the umbrella of U.S. government agreements with selected foreign governments, CIEE administers a series of reciprocal student worker agreements. These agreements allow for the mutual exchange of students seeking short-term paid employment. Students must apply for the work permit before they depart from the United States and must be enrolled undergraduates (or within six months of having graduated). The permit cannot be obtained overseas. The cost is $200.

Opportunities for three- and in some cases six-month work permits exist for any time of the year in Australia, Britain, Canada, France, Germany, and Ireland, and in the summer in Costa Rica, Jamaica, and New Zealand. Although CIEE provides job banks and assistance in applying for a job and interviewing, students must find the job and a place to stay, largely on their own. For basic information, eligibility, criteria, and application forms, see the CIEE Work Abroad brochure from CIEE Work Abroad, telephone: 800-INTL-JOB or e-mail: wabrochure@ciee.org. Also, for the U.K., phone BUNAC at 800-GOBUNAC, or e-mail to bunac@easynet.co.uk.

Outside of arrangements such as CIEE's or BUNAC's program, finding a suitable work or volunteer position in another country is almost always a complex matter. Your son or daughter is likely to need informed help from others both here and abroad. The primary obstacles are:

■ *National legal barriers.* All countries require foreigners to have a work permit, which is seldom easy and at times nearly impossible for an outsider to acquire. Students who enter the country with student visas are almost never allowed to change their visa status to obtain a work permit.

■ *Long-distance job search.* Finding out what jobs are open in advance of going overseas, communicating one's qualifications, and being interviewed are all more difficult at a distance.

■ *Earning enough to live on.* Unless one has the means to support oneself, there is the matter of pay, which may or may not be sufficient to defray the cost of travel, room, board, and other necessities, at least until one has a job. Needless to say, doing volunteer work or securing an unpaid internship may require even more financial support, even if one receives a token salary, as is often the case.

Students seeking some practical experience overseas in addition to credit for their academic studies may do so by means of an internship, almost always unpaid. Internships may be set up as a formal part of an academic study abroad program (in which case some credit may be earned), or as something apart from the formal program, as an extracurricular activity, in which case receiving credit is more problematic. More and more programs recognize that students seek such opportunities. If the possibility of an internship is not mentioned in program materials, do not conclude that it will be impossible to arrange one. Often program directors are willing to work with students who would like to supplement their formal studies with other less formal learning experiences abroad.

A Note on Safety

Parents are understandably concerned about the safety and security of their children, wherever they may be, but the prospect of a daughter or son being thousands of miles away in a foreign land may foster new levels of apprehension, leading to questions such as the following.

■ Is traveling and living in another country inherently more dangerous than staying home?

■ Are some countries safer than others?

■ Within a single country or region, are some programs or program types safer than others?

■ In choosing a program, what can and should students and parents be able to expect by way of assurances about safety and security?

■ How can parents help to minimize risks and maximize the safety and security of their children?

Study abroad programs cannot guarantee the absolute safety of participants or ensure that risk will not at times be greater than at home. Nor can they monitor the daily personal decisions, choices, and activities of individual participants any more than is the case on the home campus; prevent participants from engaging in illegal or risky activities if they ignore rules and advice; represent the interests of participants accused of illegal activities, beyond ensuring that legal representation is available; assume responsibility for acts and events that are beyond their control; or ensure local adherence to U.S. norms of due process, individual rights, political correctness and sensitivity, relationships between the sexes, or relations among racial, cultural, and ethnic groups.

However, most overseas study programs recognize their responsibility to do their utmost to provide a secure and unthreatening environment in which your son or daughter can live and learn in a safe and secure environment. Responsible campuses and programs consult regularly with colleagues around the country who are involved in the administration of study abroad programs; with resident program directors of programs; with responsible officials of foreign host universities; with contacts in the U.S. Department of State and other agencies; and with other experts who are well-informed on issues and events.

The ability to communicate almost instantaneously worldwide via fax machines and e-mail also enables campuses (and parents) to obtain and share information quickly and accurately in the event of an overseas emergency that may have repercussions for study abroad programs and students.

Most campuses and programs have in place an effective system of consultation that enables them to make timely decisions concerning the safe operation of their programs. Moreover, every study abroad program should have in place guidelines for promoting student safety and for responding to emergencies. Feel free to ask for details of such plans from the programs in which your son or daughter is interested. More information on living safely abroad is offered in Part 5 of this book.

On the matter of personal safety and security generally, it is useful to take a comparative perspective: The United States is known around the world as a comparatively dangerous country, and our street crime statistics back up this view. No country has as many guns in the hands of private gun-owners nor as many gun-related injuries and deaths. U.S. rates of drug and alcohol abuse are among the highest in the world. Although tourists and other international visitors (including 460,000 degree-seeking students) come in great numbers to visit the United States, many arrive concerned about what they think they will find.

Yet, the perception that life at home is still safer than life "over there" leads some to conclude that maybe our students should stay home, "where they belong." U.S. media coverage of the rest of the world focuses, often sensationally and melodramatically, on overseas political upheavals, violent strife, and natural disasters, rather than on positive political and social developments or on the richness and human warmth of life as it is actually lived. One of the first responses students who study abroad have to their overseas environment is how "normal" life seems and people are, in spite of cultural differences. That discovery comes when they sweep away stereotypes and misperceptions, seeing things with their own eyes.

Parents, students, and study abroad programs all have a role to play in minimizing potential dangers. A sober and realistic assessment of safety risks associated with any region, and the study abroad programs that take place there, is therefore strongly advised. Parents should be duly skeptical if a program or institution suggests that its offerings are completely free of risk, or if its representatives seem unwilling or unable to discuss the risks involved.

Among the responsibilities of program providers are to conduct periodic and ongoing assessments of safety conditions at the program site, excursion sites, and at nearby tourist destinations; to provide comprehensive safety information to enable prospective applicants to make informed decisions about participation and about their behavior while on site; to orient participants to help them avoid high-risk situations and deal better with problematic events; to take appropriate action if the local safety environment deteriorates; and to refer participants experiencing difficulties to appropriate medical, psychological, or legal help.

Participants, too, have their responsibilities, among which are to make available to the program any information that will be useful in planning for their study abroad experience; to read and evaluate all materials issued by the provider that relate to safety, health, legal, environmental, political, cultural, and religious conditions at the site; to conduct their private life in a prudent manner, paying particular attention to local conditions as outlined by the program; to assume responsibility for the consequences of personal decisions and actions; and to purchase and maintain appropriate insurance and abide by the conditions imposed by the policy.

Parents, too, should obtain and evaluate safety information concerning the study abroad location, be involved in their offspring's decision to participate in a particular program, and engage their children in a thorough discussion of safety and behavior issues linked to the overseas program and related travel and activities.

Specific measures students overseas can take for minimizing danger and the risk of crime are offered in Part 5 of this book

Researching Study Abroad Options

Students are on campus on a regular basis, whereas parents are not, and communications between parents and students are often less than ideal. Students seeking out information about study abroad generally and about particular programs usually have ready access to information from the following sources.

■ *The study abroad library on campus.* Staffed by advisers and containing information on institutional policies, scholarships, fellowships, and grants, the library will stock general guides and reference books describing thousands of program offerings, as well as detailed brochures and catalogs for individual programs. The library may also make available program evaluations completed by past participants; magazines such as *Transitions Abroad*; videos, films, slides, and photos on programs; foreign university catalogs; and access to the World Wide Web and education databases. Often direct connections exist with programs overseas, enabling students to talk with overseas staff and students abroad.

■ *Campus advising and support services.* Study abroad advisers and faculty members are available for one-on-one and group sessions with interested students. They provide referrals to other campus offices (financial aid, registrar, etc.) as necessary.

■ *Campus meetings and study abroad fairs.* Informational meetings are held periodically for anyone interested in studying abroad, as well as for students interested in particular countries or regions, languages, or disciplines. Representatives of organizations that offer study abroad programs to students from participating colleges and universities (known as consortia) visit the campus occasionally to discuss their programs. Representatives of various study and work abroad programs will attend study abroad fairs organized by the college or university.

■ *Program materials by mail.* Students may send for materials and applications directly from program sponsors.

■ *Returned students.* One-on-one or group information sessions allow students to hear from past participants about their experience.

Most campuses welcome parents who wish to use such resources, but they are set up primarily for students, and logistical difficulties make it impossible for most parents to spend much time on campus. This suggests that much of the ground work needs to be done by students, who should be encouraged to share their preliminary findings and inclinations with you. The key is to establish a balance between a student's need to reach a mature and independent decision and the family's need to understand the reasons behind the decision and its full financial, academic, and logistical implications.

Earning Academic Credit

■ How is credit awarded in general, and how does the practice differ when a student studies abroad?

- Can my son earn credit in his major? Elective credit? Graduation credit?

- What are the procedures used for awarding credit from programs sponsored by my daughter's home campus?

- Can credit be transferred from other study abroad programs? From foreign universities? What is the process like?

- Are grades earned overseas factored into the GPA?

If your son or daughter is enrolled in a study abroad program approved by his or her home campus and remains a U.S. degree-seeking student while enrolled overseas, the prospects of earning academic credit are very good. Furthermore, all registered students taking a full load of courses overseas qualify for federal financial aid should their economic circumstances warrant it. Credit for courses taken in any program can usually be counted toward degree studies and sometimes toward the satisfaction of academic major or minor requirements. This is far from automatic, however, so it is important to understand fully what is involved.

The term "academic credit" has no universal meaning, nor are there any national (much less international) standards for awarding it. Whether or not students actually receive credit for their formal studies overseas depends on two considerations: (a) judgments made in advance (and sometimes also in retrospect) by their home institution about whether the courses taken overseas meet the standards and policies of the home institution; and (b) the quality of students' academic performance, as judged by teachers of the overseas courses. Doing well in the course work is the second step; the first is making sure that the courses themselves are of a quality sufficient to justify the award credit by the home campus.

TYPES OF ACADEMIC CREDIT

Home Institution Credit

If students enroll in a program sponsored by their home institution, the courses are by definition of a standard that will earn credit, so the only question lies in academic performance. The courses students take in such programs should be listed in the college catalog. From this it will also be clear what sort of credit — graduation, elective, major — is possible. This is usually the case whether the home institution provides the instruction or it is offered through an overseas host institution or agency.

Transfer Credit

When students enroll in a program not directly sponsored—though still perhaps formally approved in advance—by their home institution, the courses they take and the quality of their performance will usually be evaluated by the home campus through its normal procedures for handling "transfer credit." The individuals at your son's or daughter's institution who are likely to be involved in the decision over whether or not to award transfer credit include the registrar, faculty, and overseas studies personnel. The process usually involves examining records that must be furnished by (a) the overseas institution that does the teaching and grading; or (b) by another U.S. college or university, or consortium of universities, that sponsors the program and provides credit recommendations. In addition, students may be required to furnish supplementary evidence of their studies—papers, tests, journals, and so on.

Credit by Examination

It is sometimes possible to earn credit by taking and passing written or oral examinations of what has been learned overseas administered by the home institution. This practice is quite frequently followed to assess language proficiency or gains in other skill areas, for example, in the performing arts, in social science research, or in field science. Sometimes there is a charge for the testing or the credit. Inquire about the policy and precise charges in advance—usually by contacting the registrar's or bursar's office.

Credit for Work, Internships, and Volunteer Service

As discussed elsewhere, few colleges or universities grant credit for travel alone or simply for living overseas. But if your daughter's or son's college gives credit for domestic off-campus work or service, it may also give credit for similar activities overseas. If this is the case, it is important for all concerned to learn what needs to be done beforehand to qualify for such credit. Almost always, it requires finding an adviser who will oversee and evaluate the overseas experience and activities. Frequently, in addition to whatever students actually do overseas, they will be asked to keep a journal, write reports, do additional readings, conduct interviews, and in general demonstrate that they have done some serious reflection on the meaning of their activities.

"PREAPPROVAL"

Almost all campuses have procedures and policies in place for preapproving program selection, participation, and credit. This protects both the institution and the student. It is important for the institution to give students clear guidelines and standards for earning credit for study abroad so as to minimize misunderstandings after the fact. It is important for you and your student to know in advance what is and is not possible. No two institutions have the same policies and practices. Further, preapproval is not just a matter of deciding whether or not earning academic credit is possible in general, but of determining what sorts of credit and at what levels—graduation credit, elective credit, upper- or lower-division, and major or minor credit. What has in fact been preapproved for credit and at what level(s), pending the successful completion of the work, should be made clear to students and parents alike.

Your son's or daughter's college may have a list of other programs that are preapproved for credit. If it does not, or if your son or daughter wishes to enroll in a program not on this list, there is probably some sort of review and approval process set up by the study abroad office and conducted by an adviser in consultation with faculty. It is never advisable for a student to leave campus without clear written assurances that upon successful completion of overseas course work the credit he or she expects to earn will be granted. Except at institutions whose policy it is never to preapprove courses, students' chances of earning credit after they return, without preapproval, are usually minimal.

Preapproval typically involves the following steps:

- Getting the appropriate faculty members to agree to the chosen courses. Most campuses have a form for this. The signature indicates the faculty member's belief that the course content at the overseas institution or site is "creditable" toward graduation. To know whether the course will count toward requirements of the academic major, the student will need to consult with his or her major adviser before leaving.

- Making sure that the institution or program is on the campus's "approved program list" or successfully petitioning for approval of participation in the program. The study abroad office can provide advice on submitting an appropriate petition.

- Satisfying the home institution's regulations for the minimum number of credit hours to be earned during the time away to ensure steady progress toward graduation.

ENROLLMENT CHANGES ON SITE

If students make any changes in their preapproved courses, it is their responsibility immediately to provide information about the new course to the faculty member who signed their approval form. If they are considering courses in a department from which they have not received prior approval, they should keep in mind that each home department has its own requirements. Students should contact the department before committing to the new course.

GETTING A TRANSCRIPT

To receive credit for programs not sponsored directly by the home institution, students normally must have the institution responsible for the study abroad program send a transcript to the registrar on the home campus. If the institution does not issue transcripts, have it send a certificate of attendance or diploma indicating the courses taken and a written, qualitative evaluation of completed work.

Students usually must complete a full load of courses as defined by the foreign institution and their own. The equivalent of a C- or better is usually required to receive credit. Some institutions may accept a D grade, however, as institutional policies on grading and grade transfer vary widely. Your son or daughter should know, in advance, the policy of his or her institution, and this should also be made clear to parents.

POSTAPPROVAL

In certain cases, students will need to seek approval for their courses after the fact. This is applicable if they have:

- Taken courses for which they received no prior approval

- Taken courses under the aegis of departments that will not grant credit until appropriate faculty members examine the course descriptions and the work performed

- Taken courses for which students want credit toward their major.

Again, each situation may require evidence of work, including papers, exams, notes from oral presentations, or portfolios. While it is not impossible to get postapproval—and in some cases this is the only way an institution awards credit—seeking preapproval is always the better alternative.

Because further questions about credit might arise later, students are well-advised to keep all of their records from abroad—including syllabi, exams, papers, notes, projects, and portfolios—and be ready to present them to faculty and administrators if asked to do so.

The Costs of Study Abroad

Anything international or foreign is associated in the minds of many parents with high costs. You might therefore assume that the participation of your son or daughter in a study or work abroad program is a venture you cannot afford. But does study abroad in fact cost more than on-campus study? How does one find out what is covered and what is not?

What study abroad costs depends on the many possible variations and permutations of:

- Program sponsorship

- Institutional tuition policies

- The applicability of financial aid

- Program duration

- Program location

- Travel costs

- The strength of the U.S. dollar

- Other personal and institutional considerations.

The range of expenses can vary from somewhat less than to much more than domestic study, depending on timing, institutional policy, and program selection. Once a program is selected, there are things you can do to limit additional costs, not the least of which is to work with your son or daughter to establish and maintain a realistic overseas budget.

Many U.S. institutions do their best to make study abroad expenses roughly equivalent to the costs of home campus study so as to encourage overseas study as a viable option for all students. As a result, the opportunity to live and learn in another country can generally be paid for using the same set of financial resources that are assembled to pay for domestic studies This is not always the case, unfortunately, particularly at institutions where some categories of financial aid (e.g., private institutional grants) cannot be used abroad.

VALUE FOR MONEY

The challenge to parents and students is to find the right balance between program value and the money available. Program quality and cost may be integral, somewhat related, or have little to do with each other. Qualitatively similar programs in the same city or country may, for example, vary in cost by often surprising amounts, depending on whether they are sponsored by a private or public institution. Or they may vary in what they provide participants. One may be bare bones: direct enrollment in a foreign university, little on-site support staff to help with orientation or accommodations, and no language training or special courses for foreigners. Another may offer creature comforts, excursions to sites of historical and cultural interest, a full orientation and cross-cultural counseling, e-mail access, hotel-like rooms and food, a student center for social activities, a full-time resident director and staff, and more. Yet the low-cost program may still provide students with the essential academic and experiential education they seek, and sometimes even promote greater maturation and independence.

The Costs of Study Abroad

Before signing on to any program, you should have accurate figures, or at least solid estimates, of the following costs:

GENERAL

Application fee

Program deposit: Is it refundable? Under what conditions?

Instructional materials: books, supplies, labs, computers

Program fee: What does it cover?

Program-related excursions and other cultural enrichment activities (unless included in program fee)

PRE-DEPARTURE

Passport fee

Visa, if required

Medicine, inoculations, immunizations, etc., often a sizable item when preparing for travel to developing countries

Medical and dental examinations prior to departure

Traveler's insurance for lost or stolen personal items

International Student Identity Card

Luggage or backpack that is convenient to carry

Appropriate clothing for the climate and for traveling comfortably

TRAVEL

International airfare (sometimes included in program fee, but usually not)

Commuting costs to and from campus

Independent travel

In-country domestic transportation between the point of international entry and program site (sometimes covered in program fee, but not always)

LIVING EXPENSES AND MISCELLANY

Room (arrival to departure, not just for duration of formal program)

Food (all, not just some, arrival to departure)

Computer and Internet use fees

Books

Housing or key deposits

Residence permits

Other (laundry, cleaning, postage, incidental expenses)

In addition, you must take into account the costs of your son's or daughter's social life, of gifts and souvenirs, and of mail and other long-distance communications. Some such things will amount to less than what he or she now spends on campus, and some will cost more. Past participants or program representatives can help with these estimates.

It is useful to learn how to estimate the inclusive costs of competing study abroad programs. Distinguishing costs that have their basis in the home institution from those that are incurred overseas is one way to begin your calculations. The table at right should help.

OVERSEAS COSTS

Overseas costs can vary dramatically by continent, country, urban or rural environment, and the strength of the U.S. dollar against foreign currencies. The cost of living in western Europe is more than the cost of living in Latin America—Spain is far more expensive than Mexico or Belize. Costs vary by location within a country or region, as well. Paris is a more expensive place to live than a village in the Massif Central. On the other hand, a program in a South American capital, such as Buenos Aires or Santiago, is likely to be somewhat more costly than a program in rural Spain.

In all cases, it must be understood that some administrative expenses are incurred by the home institution in providing professional advising to students, making program and cross-cultural information available, holding predeparture meetings, producing promotional materials and guides, and paying the salaries of faculty and staff to direct or otherwise implement the program. These costs may not be apparent from program materials, but they are nevertheless very real to institutions.

U.S. INSTITUTIONAL COSTS

Some institutions, private and public, charge full home-campus tuition (and possibly room, board, and fees) for participation in programs they sponsor, including direct exchanges with foreign institutions whose tuition may be far less, and often for participation in any other program. In effect you are paying for the cost of home-campus credit.

Other institutions ask participants to pay an administrative fee, which may be large or small. Some campuses assess one fee for their own programs, and another for other programs. Other institutions charge their students nothing for participation in externally sponsored programs; students pay only the program sponsor. Some institutions charge students for transferring credit from a program that has not been preapproved.

COSTS BY PROGRAM TYPE

As touched on above, costs vary by program: Some programs include more features, better support services, and more on-site supervision than others, and some take place at institutions that charge more tuition or higher room and board than others. Immersion and direct enrollment programs tend to be cheaper than island programs, especially if additional language instruction is not required. As a rule, the more that needs to be done to provide special courses or support services for students, the more it will cost. Students can save by thinking carefully about what sorts of services they really need. Parents can help by making sure the student is being realistic about his or her needs.

COSTS BY PROGRAM DURATION

Costs obviously increase with the length of the program. You should be aware, however, that there are economies of scale, so that, for example, a year-long program rarely costs twice as much as a semester program, since fixed administrative and travel costs are spread over a longer period of time. Likewise, summer programs, when travel is taken into account, can cost almost as much as quarter or semester programs, and often financial aid is harder to get.

WHAT'S COVERED BY THE PROGRAM FEE?

Most program materials will list a program fee. You should make sure that this is the fee you will be expected to pay, not one for last year or an estimate.

With the help of your son or daughter, you should read the materials carefully and ask questions of your son or daughter, campus officials, and program sponsors until you become absolutely certain what is and is not covered by this figure. An aggregate figure may be stated, but you should read the fine print carefully.

Be especially alert to when the program formally begins and ends in relation to your daughter's or son's arrival and departure, and whether room and board during vacation and holiday periods are covered. Students who enroll directly at a foreign university and live in university residence halls may find that the residence halls close during the long breaks and that they must cover their room and board during those periods.

Room and board is an especially tricky matter. Many programs do not offer a full board plan. If students have facilities and equipment to do some of their own cooking, what is the cost of food and other preparations? If students have to eat out, what sorts of facilities will be available to them and what is the cost of an average lunch or dinner?

Programs in which students spend time in the home of a local host family often offer only partial board with the host family, so other meals must be purchased unless the program covers the costs of some or all of those meals. Find out how many meals your son or daughter will be responsible for. Find out if students will be permitted to use a host family's kitchen to prepare any meals that are not included. In some countries, it is unheard of to allow guests to use the kitchen.

Admissions

Applying for admission to a study abroad program will seem familiar to parents and students, and indeed the process has much in common with applying to college. For some students and parents one and only one program will seem right and only one hit-or-miss application is completed. For others, it may make more sense to apply to two or more comparable programs.

It is absolutely essential that the application be complete (or at least that missing portions be promised and in timely transit) and that it be submitted on time. Deadlines are important and usually reflect a variety of internal priorities that cannot be much delayed. Getting the application completed and in on time is of course a student responsibility. But parents can keep themselves informed of the process and perhaps offer some prompting, as needed.

Applications commonly consist of biographical information, a statement of purpose, university transcripts, letters of recommendation, an evaluation of language ability, approval from the home campus, and an application fee. In addition, an interview may be required. Most programs seek candidates with a solid academic record, maturity, flexibility, good reasons for going abroad, and solid recommendations from faculty. Many choices are available to students with a grade-point average of 3.0 (B average) or better; it becomes more difficult to find programs that will admit a student with a GPA of 2.7 or less.

If your son or daughter is not admitted at once, try again, perhaps contacting the study abroad adviser first to get some counsel on the school's record with the program and to determine if another try is worth the effort. It is also possible to contact the program itself to see what the perceived weaknesses were and to ask if there are ways of strengthening the application before resubmitting it.

When a student is accepted, a deposit to secure a place in the program is usually required by the program sponsor. The payment may be as little as $100; usually it is more. Failure to make this deposit on or before the stated deadline is serious and often cannot be made up by a later payment. Parents of students receiving financial aid should immediately contact the campus financial aid office, first, to see about the overall financial aid package that will be possible, and, second, to see if the deposit can be waived until the amount of financial aid is known.

Financial Aid

Does the financial aid your family is currently receiving apply to overseas programs? This section summarizes very briefly how financial aid works for domestic study and then discusses how and why overseas study is different. By understanding what is and is not possible parents can be most effective in working with institutions to obtain the maximum amount of financial assistance. Obviously, there will be major differences between public and private colleges and universities. Some institutions will be more helpful and supportive than others.

The amount of financial assistance available to families of students wishing to study abroad is likely to depend on one or more of the following considerations.

■ The financial aid package currently being received for home campus study—institutional, federal, state, foundation, etc.

■ The commitment of the student's home institution to fostering study abroad opportunities for undergraduates and extending financial aid to such participation

■ The economic ability of the home institution to support such a commitment

■ Since inclusive study abroad costs may differ (higher, usually, than on-campus study), the amount of additional aid for which students headed overseas might qualify

■ Full-time enrollment and participation in an approved program that can be defended as part of degree studies

■ Additional scholarship aid that may be available from private or public sources.

Parents and students will usually benefit from working as closely as possible with the campus financial aid office. At the very least your son or daughter should make an appointment with the individual responsible for processing aid for study abroad as soon as he or she becomes serious about overseas study. The study abroad adviser on campus can provide encouragement, guidance, and possibly information on scholarship help.

FEDERAL AID

By far the largest and most available form of assistance for study abroad, as for domestic study, is federal aid supplied through Title IV of the Higher Education Act. If your son is taking a full course load in a study abroad program approved by his home institution and is expecting to earn credit toward his degree, the Higher Education Act, as reauthorized in 1992, states that he is eligible for the same amount of federal aid for which he would be eligible if he were studying in the United States. Furthermore, some of the additional costs of overseas studies can be taken into account when campus officials revise the aid package. All course work to be taken overseas must be preapproved for direct or transfer credit if it is to be eligible for financial aid.

The federal aid package may be made up of one or more of the following:

- Grants and scholarships (for example, Pell Grants and Supplemental Educational Opportunity Grants)

- Work-study funds (although only if the home institution runs its own overseas programs and is qualified to employ students on site)

- Educational loans (Perkins and Stafford loans, Federal Family Educational Loans, PLUS loans for parents, and the new Direct Loan)

Repayment of all loans is still usually deferred until after students graduate.

If the conditions stated above are met—participation in an institutionally approved program with the legitimate expectation of using credits earned toward that institution's degree—it is now considered *illegal* for an institution not to process federal aid for which a student is formally qualified.

Students who go abroad to participate in worthwhile educational programs such as internships, field experience, and volunteer activities are not able to use federal financial aid in support of their activities unless the home institution awards academic credit for such participation. If an institution awards credit for domestic outreach programs of this sort, it might be willing to consider extending credit and therefore financial aid to similar activities overseas. It is a possibility that may be worth asking about.

STATE AID

Some states have loan and grant programs. These differ, so check in your own state, even if your son or daughter is attending college in another.

INSTITUTIONAL AID

Institutional aid is funded by your son's or daughter's home institution, based on need, merit, or both. It is different from federal aid processed through the institution. Institutional aid is provided from institutional resources and is most often awarded in the form of scholarships or tuition reductions.

Institutional assistance is awarded only to students enrolled at the institution and sometimes is expressly restricted for use on the home campus or in the home state. A variation on this theme is to restrict institutional aid for study abroad to students participating in programs sponsored directly by the institution or formally affiliated with it. Students participating in other programs may be told that the institutional aid they receive cannot be used in connection with other programs.

Students and parents may question the rationale for such policies, especially if they seem to contradict institutional statements in support of globalization. The fact is, however, that many institutions have no choice but to restrict the amount of institutional aid that can be used for off-campus study.

On the other hand, some study abroad programs cost considerably less than home campus study. Therefore, unless your child's education is heavily subsidized through private institutional funding, study abroad may still be affordable without institutional aid through a combination of student and family contributions and federal and state aid.

A small but increasing number of study abroad programs offer need-based financial aid and merit scholarships to augment the financial aid a student may already receive from the institution. Awards from the study abroad program are generally small, but an extra $500 to $2,000 can help families justify the additional burden of study abroad.

Scholarships

International scholarships given by certain foundations and agencies may be used for study abroad. The challenge is to identify this funding well in advance, apply for it by the stated deadlines, and then, if it is awarded, make the essential adjustments in your son's or daughter's study abroad budget.

Most study abroad offices have on their shelves at least some of the books that describe scholarships available for undergraduate study abroad. Unless you can get to the campus, however, your son or daughter, with the assistance of the study abroad adviser, will have to do the basic research to identify leading possibilities. A World Wide Web resource that parents can access directly from home or work is The Financial Aid Information Page (http://www.finanaid.org). This source lists general information about aid and gives counsel on finding aid, with a special section on financial aid for study abroad. The University of Minnesota Online Study Abroad Directory (http://www.istc.umn.edu/OSAD/ Scholarship-search.html) has over 200 relevant entries. These two sources represent a good overview of aid sources and a good starting point for more specialized searches. In addition, on-line students have access to a Web site called "fastWeb" (Financial Aid Search Through the Web—http://www.student services.com/fastweb), which searches a database of more than 180,000 scholarships and loans.

Certain private organizations, businesses, churches, fraternal orders, cultural heritage groups, credit unions and others award scholarships that may be used for study abroad. Qualifying for them may depend on a student's strong academic record, but more often it is a matter of having a personal background that matches the organization's interests. Other organizations seek students with a certain academic focus, major, or intended career path.

Special attention might be paid to such organizations as Alliance Française, Goethe Clubs, the Dante Alighieri Society, and the League of Latin American Citizens, which have modest programs to aid students who study or do research in their country of heritage or interest. Rotary International has a yearly competition for students engaged in study or research abroad. The Council on International Educational Exchange offers a limited number of travel grants for students studying in developing countries; it also offers small grants to minority students from its Robert Bailey Fund. In addition, some universities and agencies that sponsor study abroad programs give tuition-reduction scholarships to a limited number of qualified students enrolling in their programs.

Some U.S. colleges and universities will reduce the aid they provide to students who receive funds from an outside source.

NATIONAL SECURITY EDUCATION PROGRAM (NSEP)

The federal National Security Education Program is relatively new. Its title refers to the original source of the money, a peace dividend from Defense Department monies now used to promote U.S. national security by increasing our understanding of the rest of the world. NSEP provides about 300 undergraduate scholarships annually, plus about 200 fellowships for graduate students and some institutional grants. Award criteria are weighted in favor of students from nontraditional backgrounds who choose to study abroad in Asia, Africa, Latin America, and other regions and countries that have not traditionally received large numbers of American students, and who concentrate on learning less-well-known languages, as well as business and certain technical subjects. NSEP stages a national competition beginning with a campus screening process. Each award is intended to supplement other available financial resources up to the amount needed to ensure program participation. Study abroad offices will have further information and applications.

Competing for scholarship support can be very time-consuming for all concerned: students, parents, study abroad administrators, the financial aid office, the registrar, and members of the faculty. Applications are often long and detailed. Interviews are sometimes required. Parents can help themselves and their children with the research and by being supportive throughout this long process. They can also help by being realistic and pragmatic about prospects and discouraging their offspring from applying for scholarships for which there is little likelihood of success.

Preparing the Study Abroad Budget and Applying for Financial Aid

The extra work required to process applications for financial assistance in support of study abroad, and to ensure payment, is less onerous if your son or daughter is participating in a program sponsored by his or her own college or university. In this case, of course, the program budget will be known to the campus, and your responsibility is limited to updating family information (for example, by providing current tax records). If your son or daughter is participating in a program sponsored by another institution, domestic or foreign, or by an agency or consortium, things get a little more complicated. In such cases it becomes necessary to devise a program budget and to document the costs of the program. Because it is in your interest to state all applicable costs, you need to know exactly what is and is not covered by the fee you will pay to the study abroad program.

At some private institutions, only federal aid is processed. At others, students are advised to seek this aid from the sponsoring program (something that is possible if the sponsoring program is itself a degree-granting institution that processes financial aid for its own students). Some agencies and consortia have their own private funds to assist students, awarded on a competitive basis, on certifiable need, or on merit criteria. It is always worth asking about this.

To have approved aid disbursed, you and your son or daughter should be aware of the following:

■ Students must sign award notices, loan promissory notes, and other official forms before leaving campus.

■ Federal and most state aid cannot be disbursed more than 10 days before the beginning of the term.

■ Federal and state grants and some kinds of loans are applied to the student's account at the home institution.

■ Some other loans and private scholarships are disbursed in check form. By having your son or daughter sign a power of attorney you may pick up and sign checks, including federal loan checks.

■ Refunds must be disbursed after home campus fees are paid. Some institutions electronically deposit refunds in student accounts.

■ Federal rules set forth circumstances under which aid must be repaid if students withdraw from their studies at certain times.

■ At some point, when students are abroad, applications for financial aid for the next semester will become due, so appropriate arrangements need to be made.

Conclusion

With a little care and effort and a good deal of advance planning, it is almost always possible to identify study abroad programs that match a student's learning style and academic goals at an affordable price. Once students are accepted into a program, there remains a host of things to do prior to departure. These are the subject of the next chapter.

Part 4

Preparing for Departure

Once students are accepted into a study abroad program, they typically receive detailed information from the program sponsor about the following topics. The work students put into choosing a study abroad program pays off when notice of their acceptance arrives. In the ensuing excitement it is easy to overlook the practical matters that need to be handled before departure. Most program sponsors help students focus on the practical by providing information about the following topics.

- Program features, academic policies, calendar, courses, logistics, etc.
- Predeparture orientations taking place on campus (if home-campus sponsored) and after arrival (in all cases)
- Travel arrangements and arrival information
- Financial aid policy and forms to be filled out and returned
- Housing, overseas and upon return (not all campuses)
- Preregistration for course work following return (not all campuses)
- Leave-of-absence and other sorts of approval forms
- Overseas communications, addresses, telephone numbers, etc.
- Health care and accident insurance information
- Country-specific information (maps, brochures, etc.)
- Suggestions for further reading.

This information—which sometimes takes the form of a comprehensive predeparture handbook and sometimes is divided into several mailings—is mailed to students either at their campus or home address. Some programs make sure that parents receive everything that is appropriate to their roles and responsibilities at this stage of the process. Others do not—by design or neglect. Although many of these important matters may be of great interest and relevance, parents may have to get the pertinent information second-hand, via their daughter or son. Alternately, they may request it from the home campus or external program sponsor.

In addition to the matters listed above, there are numerous other leave-taking issues and questions concerning legal, logistical, and financial matters that parents and students may need to pursue together, before departure. These include:

- Registering for absentee voting

- Paying income taxes

- Deferring federal loan repayments

- Assigning power of attorney

- Purchasing property insurance

- Finding medical records, scheduling a medical check-up and obtaining required immunizations, filling prescriptions, etc.

- Acquiring further information from foreign embassies and consulates in the United States, many of which maintain extensive and informative Web sites

- Packing wisely and appropriately.

Required and Recommended Travel Documents

To all governments, national identity is of major importance. Travelers must be able to demonstrate their citizenship whenever asked by a national authority at the border or elsewhere. If you are not a citizen of the country being visited, you may also be asked to show your purpose for being there. What follows is a guide for your daughter or son to follow to obtain the essential documents needed for trouble-free travel and return. The same information is likely to be furnished by most programs, but students may need some assistance or prompting from parents to set the application process in motion as soon as possible.

PASSPORTS

All travelers between countries must have a passport. A U.S. passport officially identifies a citizen of the United States. It is issued by the Department of State and is good for a period of 10 years (5 years for those under 18). All travelers must have a valid passport on their person to show border and customs authorities when they enter or leave the United States, when crossing most other

national borders, and on various other occasions that require official verifica-
tion of one's citizenship. These days, there are some exceptions to the otherwise universal requirement of a passport, for example, between the United
States and Canada, between various European nations, and within the Nordic
countries. But it is best to assume that your son or daughter will always need
have his or her passport available to show.

Passports are issued at any office of the U.S. Passport Agency or by mail
through U.S. and state courts and U.S. post offices authorized to accept passport applications. For complete information, visit the World Wide Web site of
the U.S. Department of State at http://travel.state.gov/passport_services.html.
The site presents comprehensive information on applying for a passport, including downloadable forms and a list of passport agencies, plus visa requirements and other information on living overseas. Alternately, you may call the
National Passport Information Center at 900-225-5674. If your telephone
blocks 900 numbers, call 888-362-8668 and have a credit card ready to pay the
$4.95 calling charge.

If your son or daughter already has a U.S. passport that will expire before
return, he or she should apply for a new one before departing from the United
States. Do not delay applying for a passport. The process takes a minimum of
two to four weeks, and even longer in the busy season.

The passport is by far the most important legal document one needs while
traveling overseas. In some countries, foreigners are required to carry it at all
times. Your son or daughter should should follow the advice of the study
abroad program about where to keep the passport once overseas. Students are
usually advised never to travel away from their program site, and particularly
from their host country, without their passport in hand. Parents should keep
a photocopy of the passport, and the student should take another photocopy

---

To Apply For A Passport

Individuals who have never been issued a U.S. passport must submit the following documents with their application:

■ Proof of citizenship: birth certificate (from the bureau of vital statistics in the
state of birth) or a naturalization certificate (for naturalized citizens). Birth certificates must bear the seal of the state of birth; hospital birth certificates are not official and will not be accepted.

■ Two identical color photographs, 2 inches square on a white background,
taken within six months of the date of application.

■ Proof of identity, such as a driver's license with signature and photograph.

■ Fee. The standard passport fee is $60 for individuals age 16 and older.

abroad. Having a copy of the lost passport can expedite the process of applying for a new one.

Losing a passport overseas is not the end of the world, but it will seem like it to your son or daughter. Procedures for obtaining another are very complicated and often extremely time-consuming. At home, loss or theft of a valid passport should be reported in writing immediately to the Office of Passport Services. If the loss occurs abroad, your son or daughter should immediately notify the nearest U.S. consulate or embassy, and of course his or her program or institution. Theft of a passport should also be reported to local police authorities.

VISAS

A visa is official permission to enter a country, granted by the government of that country. Visa requirements and formats vary considerably, from a simple stamp imprinted on one of the pages of the passport upon entering the country to an official document with a photograph attached. For Americans, some countries require advance processing of visas, whereas other countries (e.g., those in western Europe) require no advance processing for brief visits, usually up to three months. In the latter case, visa status will be stamped in the passport upon entering and leaving the country. When accepted into a program, students usually receive information on the visa requirements of the country or countries they will visit. For some countries, a tourist visa is adequate; others may require a student visa. Your only role in all this may be to make sure your daughter or son does not delay in following instructions. Processing times for visas vary from several days to several months.

If your daughter of son plans to travel beyond the country where the program takes place, he or she should check visa requirements well before leaving the United States by contacting the nearest consulate of the countries to be visited. It is often easiest to check first with the campus study abroad office. Information on entry requirements for U.S. citizens traveling to foreign countries is available from the Department of State Web site at http://travel.state.gov/foreignentryreqs.html.

Because students may be required to submit with the visa application their letter of acceptance into the study abroad program or foreign institution, they must save those letters (or copies) and store them in a safe place until needed. Other items that may be required to obtain a visa include the passport, proof of insurance coverage, a medical report (e.g., TB and HIV reports), police record, and proof that the student has the financial resources to cover expenses abroad. The United States requires many of these same elements from international students who wish to obtain a visa to study in a U.S. university.

Visa procedures and customs requirements are different for students holding non-U.S. passports. Legal permanent residents of the United States should check with the international student office on their home campus concerning regulations for reentering the United States. It is important to verify procedures to permit reentry to the United States, especially if students might be outside the country for more than one year. International students studying in the United States should discuss with their international student adviser what they need to do to reenter the United States.

IMMUNIZATIONS

Immunizations are required for entry to some countries. They are not required for others. Requirements change periodically depending on the prevailing health conditions, so there is no substitute for checking the requirements of your son's or daughter's destination. Moreover, it is a good idea to recheck those requirements just prior to departure. Even if no immunizations are required, it may be a good idea to obtain them. If post-program travel plans include visits to other countries, it is wise to check on requirements for entry. Program sponsors should be able to provide information. Detailed health information is available in *Health Information for International Travel,* available for $14 from the Government Printing Office, Washington, DC 20402, telephone 202-512-1800, or from the Centers for Disease Control and Prevention, telephone 404-332-4559.

For travel to certain countries your daughter or son may be required to present an official record of immunizations. The organization or institution that sponsors the program can advise on what is required for entry into the country. But, if students plan personal travel to other countries before, during, or after the program, it is again their responsibility to know what immunizations are required. It is wise to have the shots before departure.

Students can demonstrate that they have had the required immunizations by having the pertinent information entered on an "International Certificate of Vaccinations," a form issued by the U.S. Department of Health and Human Services and approved by the World Health Organization. It is obtainable from your local department of health, passport offices, and from many physicians and travel agencies. It must be filled out and dated by the physician or medical clinic that provides the immunizations. It may also be available from the campus health service, which may be able to provide the needed inoculations and other assistance.

Even if your daughter or son will not travel outside western Europe, you may wish to discuss with your physician or with the program sponsor the advisability of receiving certain immunizations. Basic childhood immunizations for tetanus, polio, diphtheria, and so on should be updated before traveling anywhere abroad. Other immunizations are frequently recommended for travel to developing countries. These include immunizations for typhoid fever and hepatitis A and B. Protection against cholera and yellow fever, along with medicine for protection against malaria, is recommended for those traveling to certain parts of Africa.

PRESCRIPTIONS

If your son requires regular medication or injections (such as insulin or allergy shots), he should check with his physician for advice on how best to acquire the medication overseas. If possible—that is, if the time overseas will not be too lengthy to make this practicable—the best counsel may be to take along an adequate supply.

Because medicines sold in other countries are not regulated by the U.S. Food and Drug Administration, it is generally not advisable to buy them over the counter in a foreign country, at least not without professional medical advice. To assist medical authorities during an emergency, prescription medicines should be accompanied by a letter from the home physician giving a description of the problem being treated, dosage, and the generic name of the medication.

If your daughter has diabetes, is allergic to penicillin, or has any physical condition that may at times require emergency care (such as asthma or mild epilepsy) she should always carry some kind of identification—a tag, bracelet, or card—indicating the specific nature of the problem and spelling out clearly the steps to be taken in case she is unable to communicate this information in an emergency.

If your son or daughter is required to take a medicine containing habit-forming or narcotic drugs, he or she should take along a doctor's certificate attesting to this fact. All medicines should be carried in their original, labeled containers. To be absolutely safe and avoid potential legal problems (laws will vary from country to country) travelers should consult the embassies of the countries they will visit before they depart.

INTERNATIONAL STUDENT IDENTITY CARD

Students enjoy special privileges and discounts in many areas of the world, including reduced or free admission to museums, theaters, concerts, and cultural and historical sites. To qualify for discounts students must be able to prove their student status. The International Student Identity Card (ISIC) is sold in the United States through the Council on International Educational Exchange (CIEE). It is perhaps the most widely recognized form of proof of U.S. student status. (College and university IDs are not honored in many places, especially if they have lapsed!) Other ISIC benefits include low airfares, discounts on travel, and certain insurance coverage.

The ISIC provides a very basic medical plan that can be raised to additional levels of coverage. In the event of serious injury or death, the ISIC provides coverage

---

Obtaining the International Student Identity Card

The cost of the ISIC ($18 at the time of publication) is likely to be paid back many times over in the form of discounts. The card is valid from September 1 to December 31 of the following year and can be purchased in advance. Information on the card and its benefits can be obtained from any Council Travel office, from CIEE's web site at http://www.ciee.org/idcards/ isic.htm, or by calling CIEE at 1.888. COUNCIL.

Six hundred colleges and universities sell the ISIC directly to students, and it is furnished by some programs to all enrolled students—check with your program to make sure. To receive the card, students must bring or send a passport photo and proof that they are a currently enrolled as a full-time student, along with the application form and payment.

---

of up to $25,000 for emergency medical evacuation for treatment of any serious injury that cannot be treated overseas, as well as the repatriation of remains in case of death. ISIC coverage supplements the protection offered by other institutional and private health care plans—many of which do not cover repatriation at all or restrict such coverage overseas. Purchase of this card is thus highly recommended.

Health and Accident Insurance

Travel itself can be stressful even in the best of circumstances. Living and learning in a different physical and social environment places additional demands on one's body and mind. Adjusting physically and emotionally to a new culture can produce a temporary shock to one's whole system.

Almost every program will ask your daughter or son to fill out a medical history form, usually in cooperation with a certified physician who will be asked to sign it. Usually this occurs after acceptance into a program, but not always. Information submitted on a medical form after acceptance into a program will not result in withdrawal of acceptance. What is crucial is that the information submitted be current, accurate, and thorough, and that nothing be disguised or hidden from program sponsors. It may be harmful to your daughter's or son's health not to be fully candid at this time (or subsequently, if something serious emerges prior to departure). Anything short of full disclosure is also unfair to the program and to its other participants. Programs can assist participants only if all physical and emotional health conditions and requirements are known in advance.

Study abroad participants are usually required by the program sponsor to have adequate health insurance coverage that is fully applicable overseas. If such coverage is not absolutely required, it will always be strongly recommended. In any event, it would be irresponsible of parents to allow their daughter or son to leave home without adequate insurance. There is nothing worse than having a sick or injured child overseas and not knowing how to pay for treatment. What represents adequate coverage may be something parents need to find out from various sources: program sponsors, the home campus, or local physicians familiar with overseas health issues and systems.

Some colleges and universities have student health care plans that cover participation in their own and external study abroad programs. Others offer coverage only to students enrolled in programs they sponsor. Some program sponsors and independent agencies have special policies for overseas study. Your family insurance plan may already be applicable overseas. If not, find out whether it can be extended.

Students traveling to countries where medical facilities are below U.S. standards may wish to purchase health insurance specifically designed for individuals living in such locations. Some medical insurance plans include a 24-hour advisory service students may call to speak with western medical personnel.

Once family or institutional coverage is in place make sure your daughter understands how it works, including what to do in the case of a medical emergency. If she should require medical attention abroad, she may have to make payment at the time of treatment, since the foreign physician or clinic may not be able to process medical bills through an American insurance company. If this occurs, she should obtain a receipt to submit with the insurance claim for reimbursement upon return to the United States. It may be helpful for her to take along a few blank claim forms.

As noted above the International Student Identity Card offers add-on coverage as well as emergency medical evacuation and repatriation of remains—something which many private and institutional plans do not offer.

Civil and Legal Matters

ABSENTEE VOTING

For some students the first opportunity to vote coincides with their period abroad. Just because your son is not in the United States at election time does not mean he cannot cast a ballot. Before he can vote from abroad, however, he must be registered to vote at home. Assuming that he wishes to register in your home district, you can help by obtaining information on voting by absentee ballot. Ask the local authorities how absentee ballots are mailed abroad, because if they are sent by surface mail, they may arrive too late to be used. Remember to make note of party, ward, district, and voter registration number (if one is used). If necessary, the absentee ballot can be notarized at a U.S. embassy or consulate.

INCOME TAXES

Parents of students who are abroad for the spring semester may have to help with filing federal and state income tax returns. IRS regulations allow persons temporarily living abroad to request an extension of the deadline for filing federal income tax forms. Decide in advance which approach works best for all concerned. Students already overseas may contact the American consulate or embassy in their host country for information on their tax obligations; the consulate may have Form 1040 and other forms available; a consular officer may even be willing to help with questions. Students can file from abroad if they make arrangements with parents to receive the necessary state and federal forms.

POWER OF ATTORNEY

If your daughter's signature will be needed for an official or legal document during her absence, have her give you or another appropriate person "power of attorney," that is, power to act on her behalf. If she will be receiving federal financial aid and must endorse the check, a power of attorney is enormously useful, since it saves the time and trouble that would otherwise be required to send the check overseas, have it signed, and await its return. To execute a power of attorney, write out in detail the specific duties that the person chosen will be allowed to perform. Have your daughter take the document to a notary and have it notarized.

U.S. CUSTOMS AND DUTIES

Think ahead to returning to the United States! Students who take with them expensive items such as cameras, radios, Walkmans, CD players, typewriters, personal computers, etc. (particularly new and foreign-made items) should consider registering such items with U.S. Customs before departure. Students who do so will avoid being questioned about whether or not they are subject to any duty upon return. Contact the U.S. Customs Office for further information and obtain a copy of the publication, "Know Before You Go" (also available by writing to PO Box 7404, Washington DC 20044). Students should save sales slips for any major purchases they make overseas and intend to take home, as refunds of taxes are often possible with proof of purchase at the departure airport.

U.S. residents are permitted to bring into the United States $400 worth of foreign souvenirs and gifts duty free. An import duty equivalent to 10 percent of fair market value is assessed on imports in the $400 to $1,400 range. Over $1,400, duty varies according to the articles imported. All articles acquired abroad and in your possession at the time of your return to the United States must be declared to Customs officials, either orally (if you do not exceed the

$400 limit) or in writing. Declaration forms will be distributed during the flight back into the United States.

Personal belongings of U.S. origin taken abroad may be sent back by mail duty free if the package carries the mark "American Goods Returned" to indicate that the articles were taken out of the United States as personal effects and are being returned without having been repaired or altered while abroad. Overseas assistance on matters relating to U.S. Customs can be obtained from Customs representatives in the American embassy.

Making Travel Arrangements

AIR

Parents are almost always called upon to help make international air travel arrangements for their children. Some programs will arrange group transportation (and in some cases require it), in which case things are easy (and perhaps less expensive). Others leave this entirely up to participants and their parents, though they may recommend travel agencies that specialize in less expensive travel for students. If the latter is the case, the program will usually have a specified arrival time and place, so that all program participants can be met as a group by program staff. Although this places some restrictions on timing and can therefore add to costs, it is essential that travel arrangements be made expeditiously so that your daughter or son can be present at the designated time and place. Do not delay making reservations, especially if the travel is to take place during any heavily traveled period, such as the summer.

Students generally should purchase a round-trip, not a one-way, ticket. Students are often vague about precisely when they would like to return—most want to do some post-program tourism—but not having a return ticket usually leads to additional costs and scheduling problems. Although changing the dates of a return flight can incur a surcharge (depending on the original ticket), one-way flights may be very expensive, and students may not be able to get a return reservation that suits their needs. Flying stand-by can also be risky, although if dates are flexible, it can be an alternative. Student travel agents overseas often find good buys on one-way tickets.

Parents and students should explore group travel opportunities with agencies serving students. Group flights tend to go to the most popular destinations, so students may have to make connecting travel arrangements to get to their program site. This may still be cheaper than a direct flight at the normal fare. So-called bucket-shop ticket agents offer enticingly discounted fares that are often advertised in Sunday travel sections of newspapers. Tickets purchased through such agents are almost always for fixed times and dates and offer no flexibility. Let the buyer beware.

Some group flights require that students return with the original group on a particular date. In such cases, changing one's return date (assuming one can get a reservation) can be very costly—although it is sometimes possible to find a round-trip student ticket with a minimal penalty (e.g., $50) for changing the return date. Today's international travel industry offers a huge number of different options, fares, and rules, especially during the peak travel season. It is well worth parents' efforts to seek out the bargains, which do indeed exist. But make sure that what you end up with suits your daughter's or son's time frame, and try to preserve as much flexibility as you can.

Whatever the travel arrangements, flight reservations need to be confirmed by phone or a visit to the airline or travel agent's office a few days before departure. This is true at both ends. Your daughter or son will be responsible for the return flight. Failure to confirm can sometimes result in forfeiture of the reservation, even if it is of long-standing duration. It is also very important to get to the international departure airport, here and abroad, on time—which can be up to three hours prior to the scheduled departure time. Otherwise, the seat may be given to another passenger.

RAIL

By U.S. standards, railroads in most other parts of the world are very convenient and still relatively inexpensive. In most countries, with fewer automobiles per capita than the United States, railroads are perhaps the most widely used form of transportation. For those familiar with limited and often slow rail travel in the United States, travel by rail overseas is usually a pleasant surprise. U.S. travelers can reduce rail expenses for some countries by buying a rail pass in the United States before departure. Such passes offer almost unlimited travel for a specified period of time and may offer special rates for students, as well as eliminate the need to line up to buy a ticket.

Information and applications for rail passes (Britrail Pass, Eurail Pass, Japan Rail Pass, InterRail, etc.) can be obtained from your travel agent. These passes cannot be replaced in case of loss or theft and are therefore the equivalent of cash. They can only be purchased outside the areas in which they are valid, so your son or daughter will have to do this before departure, unless you wish to take the risk of purchasing it later and forwarding it. The passes are personal and nontransferable and will be forfeited if presented by anyone other than the person to whom they were issued. Presentation of the passport is compulsory when making use of the pass. Passes do not guarantee a seat; some trains require seat reservations for a nominal fee.

Students expecting to limit their travel to a single country should explore rail passes available for travel within that particular country. Information on such national rail passes can be obtained from the respective national railroads themselves, some of which have offices in New York.

FOOT, BUS, TRAM, CAR

Many study abroad students find that the best way to learn about their new social and natural environment is to walk around in it, or to travel as the locals
do. Walking is healthy and often leads to new and unexpected pleasures and
discoveries. Students are unlikely to have much need or opportunity to drive a
private car overseas. Depending on local circumstances, students can use mu-
nicipal buses, trams, and taxis, which in much of the world are superior to such
services in the United States. Many students rent a bike for the semester or for
certain occasions.

While renting a car is possible in most countries, it can be very expensive,
both to lease and to keep filled with gasoline. Driving a car one does not know,
on strange roads, in new conditions, with different laws and operating customs,
can also be dangerous. Thus, if your son does decide to rent a car, he will have
to learn the prevailing traffic laws and patterns of the country—which may be
no small task. All drivers must have a valid driver's license, that is, one recognized as valid in the country. Information concerning the International Driving Permit can be obtained from the American Automobile Association, National Headquarters, 8111 Gatehouse Road, Falls Church, Virginia, 22042. AAA
can tell you which countries require such a permit (many countries will recognize a current U.S. driver's license) and can also process your International
Drivers Permit.

Extensive, country-specific information on international road travel, including common hazards and tips on roads to avoid, is available from the Association for Safe International Road Travel, 5413 West Cedar Lane, Suite 103C,
Bethesda, MD 20814, telephone 301-983-5252, fax 301-983-3663, http://www.
asirt.org.

Decent to excellent public and private bus service exists in most countries in
the world, and in some it is the only way to get around. Bus quality can range
from state-of-the-art modern (with airline type seats, television, toilets, etc.) to
downright primitive, carrying overloads of passengers (and sometimes freight
and live animals). But busses are reliable, timely, and convenient for many travel
needs. They are used by all levels of society. Bus stations are located generally in
the middle of a city or other location and offer a variety of services, including
restaurants and convenience shops. Going by bus is almost always cheaper than
traveling by train. Moreover, bus routes are considerably more varied than train
links (there are always more roads than railroads) so it is possible to get to more
places, and not always in a lot more time or with less creature comfort. Buses
link capital cities, small towns, villages, resorts, airports, train stations, tourist
centers, etc. Students living in cities or even in rural areas are likely to become
very dependent on buses (or trams)—which not only answer commuting needs
but provide a varied exposure to the local citizenry.

HOSTELING

For students planning to travel extensively abroad, hotel accommodations can be expensive. Those willing to forgo the comforts of a hotel and accept certain inconveniences can save a great deal of money by staying at hostels. A youth hostel may be anything from a remodeled villa to a log cabin with extremely inexpensive overnight rates. Restrictions vary from one hostel to another. Some impose curfews, some require that you provide your own bed sheets, some have strict check-in and check-out times. Many youth hostels require that you have an International Youth Hostel Pass before you can use their low-cost accommodations.

Information can be obtained from American Youth Hostels, National Office, PO Box 37613, Room 804, Washington, DC 20013-7613, 202.783.6161, or Hostels International, Pittsburgh Council, 6300 Fifth Avenue, Pittsburgh, PA 15232, 412-362-8181. The International Youth Hostel Handbook lists locations, facilities, and telephone numbers for all International Youth Hostel Federation hostels around the globe. It can be purchased from American Youth Hostels offices.

Student hostels, which are different from youth hostels, also exist in many countries. Although they are fewer in number than youth hostels and a bit more expensive, they are cheaper than hotels and offer more comfortable surroundings and opportunities to meet traveling university students from all corners of the world. Such student hostels are usually college residence halls or other quarters used during the academic year by local university students and scholars. Visiting students can often make reservations in advance. Some student hostels offer food service and social amenities. A current International Student Identity Card may be required to demonstrate that one is indeed a U.S. college student.

PROPERTY INSURANCE

Theft and loss of property, including losses from negligence, are not an uncommon occurrence for the inexperienced traveler. Student travelers should have insurance to cover such losses. Few homeowner's property-loss insurance policies cover overseas losses—though it is worth checking whether yours does. Normally, a copy of the local police report filed at the time of loss or theft will be required by the insurer before any claim can be considered. It is also possible to obtain insurance against losses due to trip interruption or cancellation. If your local agency does not carry such policies, it might be worth asking program sponsors for recommendations.

DISCOURAGING EXCESSIVE TRAVEL

Foreign university systems, as well as semi-integrated programs based on such systems, put a great deal of the responsibility for learning squarely on the shoulders of students. Initially, your daughter or son may thus feel less academic pressure in the overseas program than she or he felt at home, and may begin to feel the itch of the travel bug. Simultaneously students become very aware of how much they can learn simply by exploring their immediate cultural environment, making new friends, and living life as the natives do. Needless to say, looking around and exploring is enjoyable and profitable. But students should not fall into the trap of thinking that because there may be less homework the academic system abroad is, in the long-run, less demanding. The demands are simply different, a lesson students must learn.

Before it is learned, however, there may be the very strong temptation for some students to take off on too much ambitious travel. Excessive travel can be expensive and, without good counsel, sometimes dangerous. Furthermore, it undercuts the primary reason for being overseas, namely to earn credit toward the U.S. degree. It might be useful for you to talk some with your daughter or son about this. Parents may be able to prevail upon their children to use common sense when developing travel plans, to keep in mind their academic commitments, and to be realistic when calculating the amount of travel they can reasonably do during their program. With careful advance planning students can satisfy their wanderlust without sacrificing the educational benefits of the program.

Communicating Internationally

One thing parents must accept when their daughter or son leaves to study abroad is that routine parent-child communications will be different. Parents and students may have to accept the fact that new barriers of time and space cannot always be speedily and economically bridged. This may even mean some blank periods in communication—not a bad thing, but often worrisome to parents who are used to frequent communications.

Letters can be painfully slow, especially because overseas events may unfold very rapidly! The telephone can be expensive and presents time-zone coordination problems. It also may be unsatisfying if one is used to ruminative and slow-paced exchanges over the phone. E-mail eliminates much of the cost of phone bills and erases the time differential. It also offers a good mix of the informality of phoning with some of the self-consciousness of writing. But e-mail requires that sender and receiver have regular access to the Internet. It will be useful for parents and children to think through the pros and cons of each type of communication.

POST

Air mail can take up to a week just to arrive in the country; getting it to your son's local address adds additional days and may take longer in countries with inefficient postal systems. If students are traveling, they will not get their mail until they return. International postage can be quite high compared to U.S. domestic rates, especially if your correspondence is heavy. Shipping packages by air can be very expensive, while surface mail (which travels by boat) can take weeks or months to arrive. In certain countries, complicated customs regulations and forms govern what can be sent or received, and there can be tariffs and tolls to pay.

Still, there is nothing like an old-fashioned letter or care package when one is away to lift spirits and make your daughter feel connected to you and home. If you are like most parents, you will especially treasure written cards and letters. Consider keeping them as something that can be given back to her after she returns as a record of her sojourn.

If your child wants to get and receive mail—and who doesn't!—remember to make sure that he or she takes along an address book full of the names and addresses of everyone he or she might want to hear from or write: family, friends, and, for more formal purposes, campus personnel. Because the time between departure and actually taking up residence in permanent quarters abroad can be delayed by travel and orientation in another location, make sure that you get any temporary addresses from your son or daughter. To lessen needless worry, remember the time it takes to get a letter, write a reply, and have it received at the other end.

TELEPHONE

It is now possible to dial international calls directly from most locations in the United States. The usual procedure is:

- Enter the international access code: 011

- Enter the country code, normally a 2- or 3-digit number

- Enter the city code, normally a 1- to 5-digit number

- Enter the local number abroad.

You can get the country and city codes you need from your long-distance carrier.

For an operator-assisted call (person-to-person, collect, credit card, or billed to a third number), follow the foregoing instructions but use 01 instead of 011 for the international access code. The operator will come on the line to ask for the information needed (e.g., the name of the person you are calling or your credit card number).

Direct-dial calls made with the 011 international access code are the equivalent of station-to-station calls. Unless you expect your son or daughter to be immediately available, this can be a bit risky. No matter who answers at the other end, you will be billed the minimum charge for the first three minutes of conversation.

Direct-dial calls are less expensive than operator-assisted station-to-station calls, which are in turn less expensive than person-to-person calls. Long-distance carriers periodically offer special deals on calling to one or more overseas destinations. Contact your carrier for the current offerings and their restrictions.

There are no minimum charges for calls placed by your son or daughter from Europe; the charge is for the exact amount of time utilized. For calls of three minutes or longer, however, the charge will usually be more than for a call placed from the United States for a comparable time period.

Another convenient option is for students to use a phone card. For further information on phone cards, contact your telephone company or long-distance carrier.

It is also possible to dial direct from many locations abroad to the United States. Should your son wish to make a direct-dial call to the United States from the study abroad location, he would simply dial the international access code used in the country from which he is calling, plus the U.S. country code (always 1) followed by the appropriate U.S. area code and local number. AT&T's USADirect is the best-known and largest "call home" system, but others exist.

When making phone calls from or to the United States, parents and students need to keep in mind that there is a time difference between here and there. If you phone France from Boston at 9:00 pm, it is 3:00 am in Paris, Lyon, and Strasbourg. The time differences to Asia or Oceania can be as much as 18 hours.

E-MAIL, THE INTERNET, AND THE WORLD WIDE WEB

Internet-based e-mail services have revolutionized international communications. Commercial providers such as America Online offer accounts in most countries. There are two great advantages to e-mail. First, it eliminates the time-lag problem, in that senders post messages, and recipients read them, whenever it is most convenient to do so. Second, e-mail is much less expensive than long-distance phoning, in that there is no per-use fee. As a result, more and more campus study abroad offices and overseas program sites offer e-mail access for their students. Such access is far from universal, however; if it is important to you, make sure your son's or daughter's program offers it. In many countries, cyber-cafes and bookstores with public e-mail and Internet access provide an alternative.

E-mail can interfere with students' cultural adjustment if is used as an umbilical cord. Another occasional problem is that e-mail can be almost too fast, tempting students and parents alike to expect instant solutions to short-term adjustment problems that must be lived through as part of the study abroad experience. Experienced study abroad advisers know that parents often receive a very lopsided view of adjustment problems, as students are very quick to call or e-mail about the most recent crisis but too rarely report back with the solution. Without knowing about the various solutions worked out by their student, parents may conclude that the experience abroad is more unpleasant than it really is.

On the other hand, parents and their offspring can take comfort in the fact that e-mail communications allow certain practical problems—such as the need for a member of the faculty at home to approve a course switch—to be resolved in days rather than weeks. Additionally, campus advisers, overseas resident directors, and others can be in immediate contact in case of an emergency at home or abroad. Parents with World Wide Web access can usually find many sources of information about the country in which their daughter or son is living, including breaking news, political developments, and even the weather.

CONTINGENCY AND EMERGENCY PLANNING

It goes without saying that emergencies, injuries, family crises, political upheavals, and natural catastrophes can happen at home or overseas at any time with little or no warning. When personal trauma or public disaster strikes, communication links are put to the test. For this reason, parents and students are advised to devise a personal contingency plan to facilitate communications and decide on next steps. Before you make your plans, however, be sure you are fully aware of the study abroad program's emergency plan by reading the relevant literature and inquiring of program representatives as necessary. All parties should have at the ready all relevant numbers for phoning, faxing, telegraphing, and e-mailing.

If the problem occurs at home, parents are advised to contact the home campus, as well as their daughter or son, so that program staff overseas can in turn be notified to provide assistance and counsel there. If the emergency takes place overseas, students are advised first to notify program staff and then their parents. Being on-site, overseas personnel may be best situated to initiate whatever response is needed. When students are traveling on weekends or over holiday periods, they should keep their local coordinator (and host family, if applicable) informed of their itinerary.

Should parents need to contact their son or daughter during travel, emergency assistance is available through the Citizens' Emergency Center of the Office of Overseas Citizens Services, operated by the State Department's Bureau of Consular Affairs. The office is open from 8:15 am to 10:00 pm EST Monday through Friday and can be reached at 202-647-5225. For emergency communication between 10:00 pm and 8:15 am or on weekends, contact the Overseas

Citizens Services duty officer at 202-634-3600 (or at 202-647-5225 on Saturdays from 9:00 am to 3:00 pm).

The Office of Overseas Citizens Services can transmit emergency messages from you, provide some service in the event of arrest or detention while abroad, and transmit emergency funds to destitute nationals when commercial banking facilities are not available. Make sure that you have at least a tentative itinerary for your son or daughter so that in an emergency you can give the State Department some idea of where to begin looking for him or her.

Budgets, Money Transfer, and Banking

The formal costs of the study abroad program are usually billed and paid in dollars prior to departure or through an extended payment plan. Once your son or daughter arrives overseas, however, on-site expenses must be paid in a foreign currency. Some financial strategies that students and parents can follow to prepare for this situation are presented below.

Remember to find out before departure exactly what is and is not covered in the program fee. This will help you calculate how much will be needed for other purposes. An estimate of out-of-pocket expenses should be available from program sponsors and past participants.

BUDGETING

Once all likely expenses are known, sit down with your son to prepare a weekly budget that will help him live within the pre-established limits by taking care of all necessities, with an allowance for some contingencies. It is dismaying— to him and to you—to run out of funds overseas, with no easy means of replenishment. The following suggestions for sticking to the budget have been collected from past study abroad participants and their parents.

- Make weekly and daily budgets and stick to them. Adjust upwards or downwards in light of initial experience.

- Quickly learn the value of the local money in relation to the U.S. dollar.

- Be consistently alert for special student rates and discounts and know what is available through the use of the International Student Identity Card.

- Take advantage of less expensive alternatives whenever possible. Cook meals (especially breakfasts) whenever possible, and use student cafeterias rather than restaurants, saving restaurants for special occasions.

- Plan entertainment and recreation around the availability of free, inexpensive, and discounted events—on campus or in the surrounding community.

■ Shop in street markets or major chain supermarkets. Avoid specialty shops and convenience stores (which add a steep mark-up). Put off making major purchases as long as possible, so as to benefit from consumer experience accumulated in the meantime.

■ Be open-minded about eating local foods and using local brands of toiletries, because they are often less expensive.

■ When traveling, stay in hostels or in modest bed-and-breakfast accommodations as opposed to hotels that cater to tourists and business travelers.

■ Take care of all belongings and safeguard traveler's checks and cash. Losses from carelessness are difficult enough at any time. They are even more troublesome abroad.

Because program participants begin their stay in an unfamiliar environment and may not be able to translate costs readily into dollars, it is easy to be misled. Students may be confronted at first with a seemingly endless array of shopping and entertainment possibilities. Advise them to go slow. With time, they may realize that there are better bargains or lower prices to be found. They may also realize that they don't really need that new sweater.

CURRENCY EXCHANGE

No traveler should carry large amounts of cash. Traveler's checks and ATM cards are safe and convenient ways to obtain local currency as needed. Be sure that your son or daughter keeps a separate record of the serial numbers of traveler's checks. Should the checks be lost or stolen, bank authorities will need these numbers to issue replacement checks.

Traveler's checks, credit cards, ATM cards, and cash all have advantages. The best strategy is to have available several forms of payment. Some will be more useful in one country than in another, but it is best not to rely completely on one form of funds.

Traveler's checks are available in the United States in several foreign currencies in addition to U.S. dollars. They can be obtained at most banks and many travel agencies. The major companies dealing in traveler's checks are Citicorp, American Express, Thomas Cook, Bank of America, and Visa. There is usually a commission on purchases of traveler's checks, but many travel agents and credit unions offer fee-free traveler's checks. Buying traveler's checks in small denominations means carrying a bulkier package of checks, but it also means that one has greater control over the amount of currency received each time they are cashed. Most experienced travelers take a combination of larger ($100 or $50) and smaller checks ($20).

It is helpful to have some local cash before leaving the arrival airport—for buses, taxis, a cup of coffee, or a snack. American currency can be exchanged for foreign currency at most international airports before departure, though surcharges and exchange rates there are among the most unfavorable to be found. In almost all instances, one does better at the international airport upon arrival, assuming there is time before heading off. It is best to avoid having to exchange currency at hotels, restaurants, or retail shops, as the exchange rate may be very bad (except in some Asian hotels). Generally, one should exchange money at major national banks or, in Europe, at railroad stations.

Banks abroad (including their ATMs) almost always offer the fairest exchange rate available. One can, however, expect to pay a commission that varies from one country to another every time one exchanges currency. In some countries the commission is based on a percentage of the amount exchanged, whereas in others a flat fee applies regardless of the amount of the transaction. With a flat fee it is advantageous to exchange larger amounts to avoid repeat visits, although this necessarily means carrying more cash than otherwise might be advisable.

BANKING

Answering the question of how to provide students with the money they routinely need when they need it is not easy. It may not make sense to take all of the money with them, unless their program is short—in which case there may be no alternative. For programs of longer duration, some of the funds, such as financial aid disbursements, may not be available at the time of departure. It is seldom easy, and in some places impossible, to establish a bank account ahead of time and deposit money in it. Most students wait until arrival in the country to establish a bank account. Their on-site program orientation should tell them how to do this. Resident staff will be acquainted with the various banks and the services they offer to foreign visitors. They should know about the different types of accounts and how to find the branch office closest to the students. Many foreign banks have their own bank cards (sometimes local, sometime national, sometimes worldwide and affiliated with Visa or MasterCard), allowing holders to make withdrawals from their ATMs.

CREDIT AND BANK CARDS

Credit cards make foreign currency transactions easy, often give good rates of exchange, and are invaluable in a financial emergency. Almost all large restaurants, train and bus stations, department stores, hotels, car rental agencies, and the like accept credit cards these days, at least in Europe and East Asia. Smaller merchants, cafes, shops, and bazaars may not, however. Some countries of the world, and parts of many others, remain cash economies in which credit cards are not widely accepted. Nevertheless, if at all possible, see that your student carries a credit card, if only for emergencies. On the down side, the loss or theft of a card abroad can be a huge inconvenience when traveling.

The three most widely known and used cards abroad are American Express, Visa, and MasterCard. Students can go to an American Express office and cash a U.S. personal check for up to $1,000 (only the first $50 will be provided in cash, the balance in traveler's checks). With a Visa or MasterCard, holders can usually obtain cash advances from a foreign bank against their domestic account. Visa and MasterCard are more widely accepted than American Express in student-type accommodations.

If your daughter has a U.S. bank card or debit/check card that belongs to an international network such as CIRRUS, she should be able to withdraw money from most bank machines in Europe, and increasingly in other regions. This is one way to obtain local currency, often at a quite good exchange rate. Where this option is available, you can deposit money in your daughter's U.S. checking account (U.S. savings accounts are generally not accessible from abroad), and she can draw on it overseas. Be sure to check the details well before departure. Your bank should be able to tell you how to find the location of ATM machines that will accept your card in various cities abroad. Make sure your daughter memorizes her PIN in figures rather than in letters; some keypads abroad lack the letters.

OTHER WAYS OF TRANSFERRING MONEY FROM HOME

Wire Transfer

Wire transfers from your American bank to a bank abroad are usually quick. They are relatively expensive, however, and may not be reliable in some regions. Your hometown bank may have to process wire transfers through an internationally recognized American bank, which will in turn deal with a comparable internationally recognized bank overseas. Your son or daughter may have to establish an overseas account to receive the transfer.

American Express Money Order

American Express money orders are relatively fast. Transactions must be initiated at an American Express office in the United States and completed at a branch office abroad. American Express can wire money to its overseas offices, as well, where it can be picked up, with appropriate identification. American Express offices are located in major cities overseas.

International money orders can be purchased at many major banks in the United States and mailed abroad to be cashed at a bank for dollars or the local currency. International money orders require no time to clear.

Foreign Currency Draft

It is also possible to obtain from an American bank a foreign currency draft against a recognized bank in the foreign country (e.g., a check in Spanish pesetas drawn against the Banco Hispano-Americano in Madrid for a student in Salamanca). In such cases, the currency exchange rate is likely to be poor. The draft can be sent to your daughter at her postal address (preferably by registered or certified mail) for cashing abroad. Even though the draft is in the local currency, getting the currency can take time. It is best to deposit the check in a local account.

Cashier's Check

If you must send a bank draft in American currency, a cashier's check drawn against a major American bank (e.g., Chase Manhattan) can be obtained from your hometown bank and forwarded via regular air mail abroad (again, use registered or certified mail). This may prove to be a relatively slow way of sending the money needed overseas, since one has to wait for the foreign bank to confirm the check's validity. Local currency exchange rates would apply.

Personal Check

Personal checks drawn against your local hometown bank may be virtually worthless because of the long time it takes each bank to clear the check. Some overseas programs make arrangements with their local bank to cash personal checks for students if the check bears the program's stamp or other endorsement.

Not all of the preceding counsel may apply in every country—indeed, it is probably more accurate for the major western European countries than for the rest of the world. Parents are advised to compare what is suggested here with what they find out from program sponsors and domestic banking sources.

Packing and Shipping

Study abroad students often report that they (a) packed too much, especially clothes; and (b) packed some things they never needed, while (c) forgetting things they could have used. Others report that they were often able to buy what they needed overseas (although sometimes at higher costs). Others buy more than they can fit into their bags, so getting everything home becomes a problem. Because people dress differently in other countries than on U.S. campuses, students may want to have the option of buying at least some of their clothing abroad, depending on how much they wish either to blend in or stand out. What they take will depend to an even larger extent on where they are going, of course,

A Packing Checklist

Although study abroad programs are generally good at advising students about what to pack, here is a unisex packing checklist to use as a general guide. It should be modified in accordance with the information provided by the program sponsor and by former participants.

CLOTHING

1 pair of rain-proof walking shoes
1 pair of flip-flops for the shower
Socks
Underwear
Shorts (may not be appropriate in
    certain cultures or climates)
Skirts/trousers
Shirts/blouses
Sweater/sweatshirt

Pajamas, slippers
Poncho/rain jacket
1 light jacket
1 bathing suit
1 hat
1–2 nice outfits
Winter coat, gloves, hat (depending on
    location and season)

MEDICINE AND TOILETRIES

Prescription medicine (carry copy of
    prescription)
Toothbrush and toothpaste
Soap and shampoo
Comb and brush
Sunscreen, moisturizers, cosmetics
Deodorant
First aid kit
Contraceptives and condoms if these
    will be needed

Aspirin
Tissues
Tampons/pads
Razors/blades
Extra eyeglasses and sunglasses
Extra contact lenses and cleaning
    solutions
Tweezers, nail files/polish, etc.
Linens (if not provided by program site)
Towel/washcloth

GIFT SUGGESTIONS

Caps, clothing, and other items with college logos
Cookbooks with American recipes (pancakes, chocolate chip cookies, etc.)
Nonperishable foods (maple syrup, peanut butter, saltwater taffy, etc.)
Cassettes or CDs of American music (jazz, folk, pop, rock, etc.)
Calendars with U.S. scenery
Pen-and-ink drawings or professional quality photographs of your area
U.S.-style paraphernalia (Disney , Warner Brothers, NBA, MLB, NFL, etc.)
Handmade crafts or jewelry (especially Native-American)

MISCELLANEOUS

Watch (cheap, reliable)
Camera and film
Flashlight
Address book; lightweight stationery and envelopes
Journal
Books, guides, maps, train schedules, handbooks
English-language paperbacks (to read and swap)
Dictionary
Day pack/small compressible knapsack
Plastic storage bags
Laundry soap and line
Hostel sleep-sack (a folded-over sheet hemmed up the side)

Money belt or neck wallet
Change purse
Umbrella
Luggage lock and tags
Battery-operated alarm clock
Moist towelettes
Batteries
Music/cassette tapes/CDs
Adapter and voltage converter with appropriate plugs (electric current and plugs in most other countries differ from U.S. norms)
Small locks for backpacks and for locking luggage to overhead train racks
American cookbook, measuring cup

DOCUMENTS

Passport and visas (plus photocopies)
Tickets and rail passes
International Student Identity Card
Driver's license (U.S. or international)
Hostel membership card
Cash, travelers checks, credit cards, calling card, etc.
Copies of the above for reporting lost or stolen cards and traveler's checks
Copy of course-approval form from home campus
Copy of letter of admission to study abroad program
Home university catalog
E-mail addresses, fax numbers, and telephone numbers for destination and for study abroad adviser, academic adviser, registrar, and financial aid office at home campus

Students should not take expensive jewelry or luxury items that may be lost or that would mark them as a worthwhile target for a casual thief or pickpocket.

on how long they are going to be there, and on the range of occasions for which they wish to be able to dress.

PACKING LIGHT

Savvy returned students usually advise departing students to pack everything they think they need to take, carry what they have packed at least three city blocks; then, depending on what they have learned from this trial run, repack accordingly.

There are also some practical limits imposed by international air-travel regulations. Most airlines operating international flights permit travelers to check only two pieces of luggage whose total external dimensions do not exceed 106 inches (length + width + depth of both pieces added together) with the larger piece not exceeding 62 inches. Generally speaking, one is also permitted to carry on the aircraft a single piece of luggage whose external dimensions do not exceed a total of 45 inches. There may be some exceptions to this general rule, but some airlines are quite particular about weight limitations. The airline or your travel agent should be able to inform you of the latest policies affecting luggage limitations.

The best advice is to travel light. For emotional comfort, your daughter or son may want to pack one or two "personal necessities," but by and large excessive amounts of clothing, gadgets, and books will soon become an unwelcome and unnecessary burden. Among bulky clothing items, take only coats and sweaters that are appropriate for the climate. Students can acquire other, inexpensive items in the host country. It the overseas sojourn is long enough to experience a change of seasons, and hence usually of weather, it is sometimes wise to send clothing and other items for the next season, via economy freight, in sufficient time to reach its destination on time. A return package of items no longer needed also make sense and reduces excess luggage on the trip home.

COMPUTERS

"Will there be access to word-processing equipment in Athens? If not, should I take along a laptop?" The question is often asked.

Although more and more study abroad programs do have computer facilities, the use of personal computers in universities abroad is not nearly as widespread as it is on U.S. campuses. In most cases, study abroad faculty do not expect to receive written work in printed form. Therefore, students need not worry about having access to a PC, but they may have to recover the lost art of handwriting! If your daughter or son is someone who simply cannot function without a PC and is willing to take the considerable risk of transporting and storing it safely, it will be necessary to acquire a converter to make the PC compatible with the electrical system in the country of destination. Optionally, he or she could consider buying a unit on site.

SHIPPING

Excess luggage can be very expensive to transport, but if you or your son or daughter feel there are necessities that do not fit within your luggage limit, there are two options:

■ *Pay to take excess luggage on the flight.* If the flight is a charter, make sure one can take excess baggage. This may be cheaper than air freight and it will arrive when they do. Do not forget that students still have to get it all from the international airport to the program destination!

■ *Have packages sent on via surface mail.* Packages of clothing should be clearly labeled as "used clothing for personal use of student" to avoid customs duty, which can be very high. Packages can be insured, although some countries assess duty on the insured value of the package. A special rate exists for books. Surface mail takes six to eight weeks to arrive. Packages may be sent before departure if you know the correct mailing address, and if you are sure they will not arrive before your son or daughter does.

Beware of shipping a trunk. Surface freight takes as long as parcel post, and you are likely to have to pay dearly for storage and delivery from the port of entry to your son's or daughter's residence.

Traveling Safely

Parents are naturally concerned about their child's safety overseas. Make plans to have your daughter or son send a postcard or telephone to confirm safe arrival and to inform you of the local address and telephone number abroad. Contact program sponsors if a private arrival confirmation cannot be made. Do not expect a call immediately upon arrival, however; students are frequently tired and distracted, and you will end up worrying needlessly.

Here are some helpful safe travel tips for students from seasoned travelers:

■ *Packing.* Don't carry everything in one place! Never pack essential documents, medicine—anything one could not do without—in checked luggage. Put them in the carry-on bag.

■ *Cash.* Never carry large amounts of cash. Make three lists of traveler's checks. Leave one at home, carry one with the checks, and keep the last in a different place, along with the receipts. For the small amount of cash needed immediately and for the first few days, use a neck pouch or a money belt.

■ *Credit cards.* Take only the cards that will be used on the trip. Keep a list or a copy of cards, numbers, and emergency replacement procedures.

■ *Insurance.* It may be necessary to contact insurance agents while abroad, so keep all relevant names, phone numbers, and policy numbers in a safe place.

- *Luggage.* Mark all luggage inside and out with name and address. Put a copy of the itinerary inside each bag. Keep a list of what is in each bag and carry the list with other documents. Mark all bags in some distinctive way, so they are easily found. Count pieces of baggage before and after each stage of the journey. Travel light.

- *Medicines.* Take everything needed for the trip, along with copies of all prescriptions and the generic names of drugs. Keep medicines in original drugstore containers. Take extra eyeglasses and the lens prescription.

- *Passport.* Carry separately from your passport two extra passport pictures, a copy of your passport, and a certified copy (not the original) of your birth certificate or an expired passport. If the passport is lost, report the loss to local police; get written confirmation of the police report, and take the above documents to the nearest U.S. consulate and apply for a new passport.

Career Strategies

The experience of being abroad has a tendency to focus student attention on what comes next. Not infrequently, students return expressing an immediate interest in going back as soon as possible. Sometimes this translates into thoughts of returning after graduation to live and work, sometimes into a more open-ended decision to seek an international career.

Here are some things returned students have suggested that departing students can do before their study abroad program to explore career options and enhance their future prospects. The ideas that follow come from a checklist prepared by Amherst College.

- Make a list of alumni living in the city or country where you'll be.

- Talk with students who have just returned from your future study site. Did any of them work or perform an internship while there?

- If yes, did they do it during the semester or after? How did they arrange it?

- Read the sections of work-abroad guides that mention the place where you will be.

- Read back issues of *Transitions Abroad* magazine and other resources that discuss what employers are seeking and how to strengthen your qualifications.

- Speak with members of the faculty, including your academic adviser.

■ *Ticket.* Make a photocopy of your ticket or list its number and all flights along with the name and address of the agency that issued it, and keep this information separate from the ticket.

■ *Jet lag.* If you are traveling east or west, try to relax and save energy during the long flight. Jet lag is a physical and psychological phenomenon that affects almost all travelers in some way. Through long years of habit, your body has become accustomed to functioning in accordance with a physiological clock based on a particular daily cycle. For at least a few days after arrival, that clock is going to be out of sync with local cycles.

Information on living safely abroad is presented in the next section of the book.

Conclusion

Once predeparture arrangements are made, the next step is getting through the time remaining before the journey begins. Students and parents are likely to have to mixed feelings of excitement and anxiety during this time. Obviously, once the trip begins, students and parents part ways. The next chapter gives parents a sense of what students will be experiencing as they adjust to living and learning in a new country.

Part 5

Living Abroad

I t is one of life's ironies that although careful preparation is always advisable and always pays off, it never readies you for everything you will encounter. That certainly is the case with living abroad. It is one thing to know that people are different, but another thing altogether to be immersed in their differences. That is why good programs offer a complete on-site orientation: Sponsors know students will really pay attention once the reality of overseas life is upon them. Parents will want to review with their offspring some of the very serious dimensions of living abroad, such as learning and observing a new set of laws and norms, staying healthy in a new environment, and developing new reflexes for recognizing and avoiding risky situations. These are all serious matters, and all worthy of at least an ounce of prevention.

Arrival and Orientation

All international travelers go through a similar sequence of steps, and students headed abroad for a study experience are no different. Once these steps are completed, students typically have the benefit of an on-site orientation to jump-start their adjustment to new surroundings.

IMMIGRATION AND CUSTOMS

Travelers entering any country from another on an international airline flight or by other means present at the port of entry or border their passport and any other required entry documents, such as a visa or proof of immunization. Passport inspection usually occurs just after entering the airport but before claiming luggage. The inspection verifies the validity of the entry documents and the length of the traveler's authorized stay. When it is over, the examining officer stamps the passport accordingly. Travelers are normally asked about the purpose of the visit and how long they plan to remain in the country. The inspection process can be unnerving at times to inexperienced and fatigued travelers, but it is generally routine and cannot be avoided. Students are advised to be extremely polite to officials and to dress neatly.

After the passport has been stamped and baggage collected, travelers usually pass through a customs inspection. A customs declaration must be made, usually in writing. This will be examined by customs officials when they look at one's luggage. Travelers' bags may be very carefully examined, and people may be detained or asked to pay duties if there are any irregularities or violations of customs regulations. Most passengers in most places, however, move through customs with no special delay or difficulty.

Customs officials can be especially suspicious of students, even more so if they are not well-groomed and respectful. Students should be warned against joking about bombs or smuggled items. Once past customs, one is officially in the country legally for the duration of the tourist or student visa. Before leaving the international airport, it is wise to purchase enough local currency to last for the next week or so. It is at this point that students who have followed the advice to pack lightly will be glad they did.

ORIENTATION

Arriving overseas and beginning the program they have been thinking about for months can, paradoxically, be a major shock for students. Although most have taken airplanes before, the experience of stepping off the plane in a foreign country will be both exciting and daunting, scary and exhilarating. Spirits will be high, but so will doubts and fears that the experience ahead will not live up to expectations. Most, but not all, programs ease this transition by meeting participants at the airport or at some prearranged arrival point, then providing some sort of on-site orientation program. The latter is likely to include some or all of the following components:

- Assistance in getting to the program site and confirming safe arrival to parents

- Social and recreational activities

- An introduction to the program, the local cultural environment, and the program's rules

- Health and safety instructions and precautions

- Some language training

- Registration with authorities

- Introductory lectures on the local culture and excursions to places of special interest

- Confirmation of registration for course work

- Setting up housing and introducing host families.

The orientation represents an opportunity for all participants to get together with program leaders and others. There will usually be a review of all aspects of the program period, plus some social activities and settling-in counsel. All programs do this differently, of course, as do foreign institutions and agencies.

Living within the Law

Students visiting another country are subject to the laws of that country, like everyone else. Those laws are likely to be different from those at home, as are enforcement and punishment practices. Students sometimes need to be made aware that American legal procedures and civil rights protections, taken for granted at home, are left behind when one leaves the United States. In particular, bail provisions as we know them in the United States are rare in many other countries, and pretrial detention without bail is not uncommon. Prison conditions in some countries may be deplorable. The principle of "innocent until proven guilty" is not found in all legal systems abroad. The best advice for students, as for any traveler, is to know the laws and obey them scrupulously.

ASSISTANCE FROM THE U.S. EMBASSY OR CONSULATE

Should students encounter serious social, political, health, or economic problems, you might be called upon to work with program administrators to seek local assistance. Be aware that the American embassy can offer only certain kinds of assistance. It will:

- Provide U.S. citizens with a list of local attorneys and physicians

- Contact next of kin in the event of emergency or serious illness

- Contact friends or relatives on your son's or daughter's behalf to request funds or guidance

- Provide assistance during civil unrest or natural disaster

- Replace a lost or stolen passport.

Remember that the primary duty of U.S. embassies and consulates is to fulfill the diplomatic mission of the U.S. government—which is not always the same thing as helping particular travelers in distress. They do not provide the services of a travel agency, give or lend money, cash personal checks, arrange free medical service or legal advice, provide bail or get U.S. citizens out of jail, act as couriers or interpreters, search for missing luggage, or settle disputes with local authorities.

It is always recommended that U.S. citizens residing abroad for an extended period have their presence and whereabouts registered with the U.S. embassy or consulate. Students on a study abroad program will normally have this done on their behalf by program staff, but this is not always true. Check to be sure.

AVOIDING DRUGS

Students should avoid all involvement with illegal drugs. Drug laws vary from country to country, but in many cases they are extremely severe, regardless of whether the drug possessed is for personal use or for sale to others.

Most prison and law enforcement officials in non-English-speaking countries will probably not speak English, the significance of which students may not fully appreciate until they are confined and feeling helpless in very hard conditions. The average jail sentence in drug cases worldwide is about seven years. In at least four countries (Iran, Algeria, Malaysia, and Turkey) the death penalty can be imposed for conviction of some drug charges. Thus students should not wrongly assume that buying or carrying small amounts of drugs cannot result in arrest. In reality, Americans have been jailed abroad for possessing as little as three grams (about one-tenth of an ounce) of marijuana.

WORKING LEGALLY

In many countries, as in the United States, holding a wage-earning job while on a student visa is strictly illegal and can be grounds for expulsion. The student or tourist visa issued in advance or upon entry authorizes only living and learning in the country, and usually only for the period of a student's formal enrollment, plus in some instances some additional time for tourism. Students are likely, in any case, to be busy enough with their studies and the other demands and pleasures of living in an exciting new place that they will not have time to work even a part-time job.

However, if your daughter or son wishes to add a paid work experience to the time away, this must almost always be arranged prior to departure, to take place either before the program begins or after it ends. It can be done legally only with a formal work permit. In certain countries, work permits are not available under any circumstances; in most others, they are very difficult to obtain.

Even in countries in which students have the legal right to work part time, it may be difficult to find a job because of unemployment or because universities do not hire student workers (the way we do in the United States). In some countries students may legally engage in very limited amounts of private employment, such as English tutoring or babysitting, to earn some pocket money during their studies, but they should not count on being able to do so.

Students whose domestic financial aid package includes work-study employment must usually find a substitute (such as additional loans) for those work-study funds when they are abroad. The only exceptions are large branch-campus programs which may keep a few slots open for work/study students (arranged ahead of time, as part of the campus financial aid package).

Living Healthfully and Avoiding Disease

The risk of becoming ill while traveling abroad depends to some extent on where one goes, but even more on making adequate preparations for the health and safety risks one is likely to face and following the medical and nutritional counsel given by on-site program directors. Even with adequate preparation, living away from one's cultural environment can cause some degree of mental and emotional stress, which, in turn, can have physiological consequences.

Wherever one goes, the key to maintaining good health comes in knowing what to expect. In developing countries, even when travel is limited primarily to modern cities and tourist areas, there is usually some risk of exposure to food or water of questionable quality. If one travels to smaller cities off the usual tourist routes and visits small villages or rural areas for extended periods of time, the risk of acquiring infectious diseases is greater, largely because of exposure to water and food of uncertain quality.

Parents can generally be assured that study abroad program sponsors are as concerned as they are about providing a healthy and safe living and learning environment. But that does not mean that there is nothing left for students and parents to do to minimize the chance of illness.

Program sponsors can usually be relied on to:

■ Be knowledgeable about health and medical care at the program site and in the country and region generally

■ Provide participants (and parents, directly or indirectly) with accurate predeparture health information, so that adequate preparations can be made (including required and advised inoculations)

■ Include health, nutrition, and medical information in the postarrival orientation, so that students know how to avoid dangers and what to do when illness or injuries occur

■ Monitor student health and remain prepared to provide counsel and assistance, as needed.

Together, parents and students should look for evidence of such attentiveness, planning, and concern in the program materials they receive. If the information you need is not there, ask questions and expect adequate answers. Parents can also help by discussing early on and frankly with their daughter or son any physical or emotional health considerations that might prevent successful participation in study abroad generally, or in the particular program being considered.

MEDICAL CARE ABROAD

Good medical service is available at or near most, but not all, study abroad locations. It is often provided by arrangement with local doctors, clinics, and hospitals. In other instances, care for major medical problems may not be immediately available, although minor diseases, ailments, and injuries can be treated locally. The on-site coordinator will help students contact an appropriate physician or other medical authority when attention is required. If program staff and medical authorities abroad are to respond promptly and effectively to situations that require medical attention, they must know each student's full medical history.

During weekend or post-program travel, students may find themselves in a variety of unfamiliar and possibly remote locations. If they are not fluent in the language of the host country, they should, to the degree possible, seek out well-trained English-speaking doctors if they need medical attention. American embassies and consulates, many large travel agencies (e.g., Thomas Cook), and a number of the larger hotels abroad will have lists of English-speaking physicians. Several well established companies, including International SOS Assistance (800-767-1403, http://www.intsos.com) and Medex International (800-537-2029, http://www.medexassist.com/education/htm), offer travelers access to reputable physicians fluent in English for a prepaid fee.

SAFE FOOD AND WATER

Again, the postarrival orientation program is likely to give sound guidelines to arriving students concerning the safety of local food and water. But, in general, in areas where chlorinated tap water is not available, or where hygiene and sanitation are poor (most of western Europe is excluded), only the following may be safe to drink:

- Beverages, such as tea and coffee, made with boiled water

- Canned or bottled carbonated beverages, including bottled water and soft drinks

- Beer and wine.

Where water may be contaminated, ice and containers should also be considered contaminated. It is generally safer to drink directly from the can or bottle than from a questionable container. Wet cans or bottles should be dried before being opened, and surfaces that come into direct contact with the mouth should first be wiped clean. If no source of safe drinking water is available, boil tap water. After allowing the water to cool to room temperature in a thoroughly cleaned container, it can be used for brushing teeth as well as for drinking.

Students who plan to be in remote areas of developing countries for hiking or mountain climbing should bring a high-quality water filter or iodine tablets for purifying water.

Food should be selected with care to avoid illness. When in areas of the world where hygiene and sanitation are poor, students are advised to avoid unpasteurized milk and milk products such as cheese, and to eat only fruit that they have peeled themselves and vegetables and meat that are thoroughly cooked. When eating out, they should eat foods that are freshly cooked and served hot.

COMMON AFFLICTIONS OF STUDENT TRAVELERS

Diarrhea is by far the most common disease travelers are likely to suffer. Since the sources of the organisms causing travelers' diarrhea are usually contaminated food or water, the foregoing precautionary measures are particularly helpful in preventing most serious intestinal infections. However, even when students follow these general guidelines for prevention, they may still develop diarrhea. It is a common affliction that usually strikes a couple of days after arriving in a new area of the world and seldom lasts longer than about five days. Diarrhea is nature's way of ridding the body of noxious agents; intestinal motility serves as the normal cleansing mechanism of the intestine.

Your family physician may be able to prescribe medication for your daughter or son to take along for relief of the symptoms. Most cases of diarrhea are self-limiting and require only simple replacement of lost fluids and salts. Fluids that are readily available, such as canned fruit juices, hot tea, or carbonated drinks, may be used. You may prepare your own fruit juice from fresh fruit. Iced drinks and noncarbonated bottled fluids made from water of uncertain quality should be avoided. It is strongly recommended that students consult a physician rather than attempt self-medication if their diarrhea is severe or does not resolve itself within several days, if there is blood or mucus in the stool, if fever or chills are experienced, or if the diarrhea leads to dehydration.

Hepatitis A (infectious hepatitis) is most prevalent in North Africa, the Middle East, and the Caribbean and is not a major threat to those whose study will be limited to Europe. However, it may be contracted anywhere (including in the United States) where living conditions are crowded and unsanitary. Hepatitis A is transmitted orally through the ingestion of contaminated food or water. Clams, oysters, and other shellfish, especially if eaten raw, are common sources of the disease in contaminated areas. Symptoms associated with the disease include fever, loss of appetite, nausea, abdominal pain, and yellowing of the eyes.

Malaria is transmitted by the female Anopholine mosquito, which is common to parts of the Caribbean, Latin America, Africa, the Middle East, and

Asia. Antimalarial medication is available and is highly recommended for those who will be participating in programs in Africa, as well as parts of Asia and South America.

Tetanus is an infection of the nervous tissue produced by a contaminated wound or injury. Severe muscle spasms are produced. If left untreated, tetanus can be fatal. Cleanliness is one of the most effective weapons to prevent tetanus. Use lots of soap and water to decontaminate a wound or injury. Tetanus immunization is available, often in combination with the diphtheria vaccine. Tetanus boosters are recommended every ten years after the initial series of three injections administered one month apart.

Should your daughter or son become ill after returning to the United States, advise your physician of all travel within the 12 months preceding onset of the illness. Knowledge of the possibility of exposure to certain diseases abroad will help the physician arrive at a correct diagnosis. Most persons who return unaware that they have contracted viral, bacterial, and parasitic infections abroad become ill within six weeks after returning from international travel. Some diseases, however, may not cause symptoms for as long as six months to a year after return.

AIDS

The AIDS epidemic is a case of its own and merits special treatment here because its reach is worldwide. Everything parents and students already know about AIDS and how it is contracted is as true overseas as it is at home. Knowing this and taking precautions, such as refraining from unprotected sex and other practices that carry the risk of infection, is the only way to ensure protection. AIDS is considerably less prevalent in some countries than it is in the United States and considerably more prevalent in others.

As the World Health Organization states: "AIDS is not spread by daily and routine activities such as sitting next to someone or shaking hands, or working with people. Nor is it spread by insects or insect bites. AIDS is not spread by swimming pools, public transportation, food, cups, glasses, plates, toilets, water, air, touching or hugging, coughing or sneezing." This is as true abroad as it is at home.

However, since students will not know their environment overseas as well as they do at home, or might not be able to control that environment to the same degree, there are some things they should think about in advance to prepare themselves for all eventualities.

■ Living overseas in certain areas may present greater risks to those who test positive for the HIV virus. Some overseas locations have limited medical facilities that cannot monitor the progress of such infections.

■ Some countries now require incoming foreigners, including students, to take the HIV antibody test if they are on a long-term stay. Check with the program sponsor. Students may need a doctor's certificate showing the results of an HIV antibody test.

■ While many countries such as the United States, Australia, Canada, Japan, and the western European countries have mandatory screening of donated blood for the AIDS virus, not all do. Students and parents should find out from campus sources, the local Red Cross, the Centers for Disease Control, or embassies about safe sources of blood overseas. In some locales, ascertaining the availability of HIV-screened blood and blood products may be difficult. The HIV infection rate

---

For Further Information on Worldwide Health Conditions

■ Centers for Disease Control and Prevention: Call 404-332-4559 or 404-332-4565 to obtain a faxed information sheet for ordering documents, then call again to have the necessary information faxed back. CDC's International Travelers Hotline is 404-639-2572. Its Web-site is: http:/www.cdc.gov.

■ The State Department's Overseas Citizen's Emergency Center: Call 202-746-5225 for information on medical, financial, or legal problems while abroad.

■ The State Department's Bureau of Consular Affairs maintains a web site that provides easy access to a wealth of information on travelers' health and safety: http://www.travel.state.gov, including links to the Centers for Disease Control and Prevention.

■ The International Association for Medical Assistance for Travelers offers information on English-speaking doctors abroad and other helpful items. Call 716-754-4883.

■ International SOS Assistance, a Philadelphia-based emergency worldwide medical and travel assistance service, provides insurance for travelers to cover emergency medical needs and other services, including 24-hour multilingual assistance in centers around the world. 800-767-1403 or 215-244-1500, http://www.intsos.com.

■ Medex International, based in suburban Baltimore, for services similar to those of International SOS. 800-537-2029, http://www.medex-assist.com/education/htm.

in certain countries is extremely high. In such locations, abstinence from sexual intercourse and other behaviors that put people at risk is advisable.

■ Some poor countries reuse even disposable needles and syringes. If this is the case, students are of course advised to avoid injections unless absolutely necessary. The Centers for Disease Control recommend that diabetics and other persons who require routine or frequent injections carry a supply of syringes and needles sufficient to last for their stay abroad—a note from your doctor to explain this is advisable. Otherwise, students should make sure the needles and syringes come straight from a package or have been sterilized with chemicals or by boiling for twenty minutes. When in doubt, ask to see how the equipment has been sterilized. Caution regarding instrument sterilization applies to all instruments that pierce the skin, including tattooing, acupuncture, ear piercing, and dental work.

Reducing the Risk of Crime, Violence, Terrorism, and Accidents

Few countries have as much street crime and the potential for stranger-upon-stranger violence as the United States, so in this sense U.S. students may be statistically safer in foreign cities and towns than they are at home. Even U.S. campuses have their share of robbery, property destruction, drunkenness, and violent behavior. Indeed, many U.S. students report upon return that they had never felt safer in their lives. This does not mean that there is no crime elsewhere, or that your daughter's or son's personal safety is ever completely assured. Minor street crime (especially pocket picking) is a fact of life in many countries, especially in crowded cities that receive regular influxes of foreign visitors.

Students living or traveling in countries that are internally unstable or at odds with their neighbors can sometimes be put in harm's way. Carrying a U.S. passport is no guarantee of safety or absolute security. In certain places and at certain times, it is possible to get caught in the midst of forms of political strife that may not be directed at foreigners but nevertheless may be very dangerous. Such risks, however, are usually known well in advance, so precautions can be taken.

With regard to the threat of terrorism, in those few sites where even remote danger might occasionally exist, program directors work with local police, U.S. consular personnel, and local university officials to set practical security measures. In such places, students will be briefed during orientations and subsequently as needed about security consciousness in their daily activities.

Simply being a foreigner makes any traveler a more likely victim of crime or accidents, but there are certain precautions that American students abroad can take to maximize their safety and minimize their risks. Following is a list of do's and don'ts that study abroad programs now urge upon students:

■ Keep a low profile and try not to identify yourself by dress, speech, or behavior as a targetable individual. Do not draw attention to yourself through expensive dress, personal accessories (cameras, radios, sunglasses, etc.) or careless behavior.

■ Avoid crowds, protest groups, or other potentially volatile situations, as well as restaurants and entertainment places where Americans are known to congregate.

■ Keep abreast of local news. Read local newspapers and speak with local officials to learn about any potential civil unrest. In the event of disturbances, do not get involved.

■ Be wary of unexpected packages and stay clear of unattended luggage or parcels in airports, train stations, and other areas of uncontrolled public access.

■ Report to the responsible authorities suspicious persons loitering around residence or instructional facilities, or following you; keep your residence area locked; use common sense in divulging information to strangers about your study program and your fellow students.

■ If you travel to countries beyond your program site and expect to be there for more than a week, register upon arrival at the U.S. consulate or embassy having jurisdiction over the location.

■ Make sure the resident director, host family, or foreign university official who is assigned responsibility for your welfare always knows where and how to contact you in an emergency. When you travel, even if only overnight, leave your itinerary.

■ Know local laws. Laws and systems of justice are not universal. Do not assume that because something is legal in the United States, it is legal abroad.

■ Use banks to exchange money. Do not exchange it on the black market, that is, on the street. Do not carry on your person more money than you need for the day. Carry your credit cards in a very safe place.

■ Do not impair your judgment through excessive consumption of alcohol, and do not fall under the influence of drugs.

■ Female travelers are sometimes more likely to encounter harassment, but uncomfortable situations can often be avoided by taking the following precautions. Dress conservatively. Although short skirts and tank tops may be comfortable, they may also encourage unwanted attention. Avoid walking alone late at night or in questionable neighborhoods. Do not agree to meet a person whom you do not know in a secluded place. Be aware that some men from other countries tend to mistake the friendliness of American women for romantic interest.

As suggested earlier, students and parents should develop a family communications plan for regular telephone or e-mail contact, with contingencies for emergency situations. With this in place, at times of heightened political tension, natural disasters, or other difficulties you will be able to communicate with each other directly about safety and well-being.

SAFE ROAD TRAVEL

Driving customs vary a great deal, and pedestrians are frequently not given the right of way. Find out which roads are safest and whether it is safe to travel on overnight trains and buses. Inquire about the safety record of various modes of transportation. Avoid renting a car unless you feel very comfortable with the driving habits of the locals. For more information on international road travel contact the Association for Safe International Road Travel. ASIRT's statisticians, lawyers, and physicians compile road travel reports on over 60 countries that are available to participating universities. ASIRT, 5413 West Cedar Lane, Suite 103 C, Bethesda, MD 20814; tel: 301-983-5252; e-mail: asirt@erols.com; web site: http://www.asirt.org.

STATE DEPARTMENT ADVISORIES

The U.S. government monitors political conditions in every country of the world. Parents with concerns about crime and security threats in a given country are urged to take advantage of State Department travel advisories. These come in three forms and are available to the public free of charge:

■ Travel Warnings are issued when the State Department decides, based on all relevant information, to recommend that Americans avoid travel to a certain country.

■ Consular Information Sheets are available for every country of the world. These include information such as location of the U.S. embassy or consulate, unusual immigration practices, health conditions, minor political disturbances, unusual currency and entry regulations, crime and security information, and drug penalties. If an unstable situation exists that is not severe enough to warrant a Travel Warning, this is duly noted.

■ Public Announcements offer information about terrorist threats and other conditions posing significant risks to the security of American travelers.

For current information, advisories, or warnings, parents can contact the State Department in Washington, D.C., 202-647-4000, or get access to the same information via the World Wide Web at http://travel.state.gov. It is also possible to contact similar services in other countries via the World Wide Web. The British and Commonwealth Office is at: http://www.fco.gov.uk/reference (or telephone 011.44.171.238.4503) for information on selected countries. The Canadian Department of Foreign Affairs and International Trade is at http://www.dfait-maeci.gc.ca.

Cultural Adjustment

It is very hard to know what life is really like in a new country or region, but it is very easy to have the illusion of knowing what it will be like—from images furnished by popular communications media, from reading, or perhaps from having met a few natives. Simply knowing about another culture, however, is not the same as knowing what it will feel like to be learning and living there. Every culture has distinct characteristics, some of which are quite evident, even to the unsophisticated. Other characteristics can be so subtle that while foreign visitors may be vaguely aware of them, making adjustments is a complex process, and one may remain uncomfortable and off balance for quite some time.

Many student travelers have trouble adjusting to foreign life because they take abroad with them too much of their own cultural baggage. Cultural baggage consists of misleading stereotypes and preconceptions about others, coupled with a lack of awareness of that part of themselves that was formed by U.S. culture. As a result, suddenly feeling like a fish out of water is not uncommon among travelers. It is in fact something that your son or daughter should be advised to anticipate. It is normal, and it usually lasts for a while.

The key for students and their parents is to understand that adjustment takes time, patience, and some understanding of how to deal with the shock of being a foreigner in a new social and cultural setting. Parents should try not to be too concerned about an early wave of negative or unhappy communications about the difficulties their offspring encounter; fortunately, students deal successfully with most such problems and grow from the experience. Some campuses and most study abroad programs will offer students some counsel on cultural adjustment, before departure or after arrival. But culture adjustment is almost always something that has to be lived through to be understood fully.

According to author Robert Kohls,

Culture is an integrated system of learned behavior patterns that are characteristic of the members of any given society. . . . It includes everything that a group of people thinks, says, does, and makes—its customs, language, material artifacts, and shared systems of attitudes and feelings. Culture is learned and transmitted from generation to generation.

The presence of the many layers of culture directly affects what it is like to be an overseas student, anywhere. U.S. students abroad often find that they are treated less as Americans than as yet another species of foreign student. Like international students on U.S. campuses, they may be viewed by locals as part of a group of short-term guest visitors, treated politely but often with distancing deference. Meanwhile, various activities may be offered to them — tours to places of cultural interest, social activities, sports, clubs, and support services — all to make their stay enjoyable. That deference can be unsettling and cause feelings of not-quite-belonging. Although in the long run such feelings may be necessary for growth, they can cause frustration and irritation.

The discomforts of cultural difference naturally provoke self-protective responses in students. More than a little de facto segregation and ghettoizing takes place at many study abroad sites, and friendships with host national students may be hard to make. Unless family stays are part of the program (and something more than a boarding house arrangement), U.S. students may not be invited into the homes of host nationals. When they return to their living quarters, they may encounter a high concentration of other foreign students. When they go to the dining hall or to the local cafes, they will also likely meet other students from other countries.

Confronted with this complex reality (which they usually do not anticipate) students may be initially confused, even disappointed. After all, not everyone wants a Big Mac in the middle of Moscow. In the long run, however, it is a challenging situation for them, one that provides invaluable lessons about the nature of social reality today.

CULTURE SHOCK

Many travelers, overwhelmed by the thrill of being in a totally new and unusual environment, go through an initial period of euphoria and excitement. This is the honeymoon phase of cultural adjustment, and it is likely that your daughter will convey this buoyant spirit in her first phone calls and letters to you.

However, as the initial, very positive sense of adventure wears off, your daughter is likely to become aware of the fact that old habits and routine ways of doing things no longer suffice. She may no longer feel free to be herself, feeling instead like a foreigner. Minor problems may quickly assume the proportions of major crises, and she may find herself growing somewhat depressed. In short, she may come to feel an anxiety that results from losing most or all familiar signs and symbols of social intercourse, a kind of psychological disorientation commonly known as culture shock.

There is no clear-cut way of avoiding culture shock. Even experienced travelers report its impact every time they arrive someplace new. But simply recognizing its existence and accepting one's vulnerability to it is an important first step. With a bit of conscious effort and patience, most students will soon find themselves making adjustments (some quite subtle and perhaps not even noticeable) that will enable them to adapt to their new environment. As long as they know in advance that they will probably experience some degree of culture shock at a certain level, they can prepare psychologically to accept the temporary discomfort and turn it into an advantage.

Culture shock is a learning experience that sensitizes students to another culture at a level that goes beyond the intellectual and rational. Just as an athlete cannot get in shape without going through the uncomfortable conditioning stage, so new visitors to a strange place cannot fully appreciate the cultural differences that exist without first passing through the uncomfortable stages of psychological adjustment.

You may hear by phone or e-mail from your son when he is in the midst of short-term culture shock. He may not recognize what is happening and may exhibit a degree of irritation or negative feelings that can be very disturbing, even alarming, to you—even if culture shock has been discussed during orientation. It will be hard not to be concerned, and surely you should give whatever comfort and support seems natural and appropriate. You should keep in mind, however, and perhaps even remind your son, that this state of mind is normal and most likely temporary; indeed, it is part of the adjustment and growing process. If you believe that the discomfort goes beyond short-term adjustment problems, you should feel free to contact the program sponsor to discuss your concerns, but in most circumstances you can help most by being a good listener, counseling patience, bolstering confidence, and expressing optimism that things will work out. Don't forget to remind him of the long-term goals of the experience.

CULTURAL STEREOTYPES

Frequently, the overseas stereotype of the American is far from complimentary: the boorish tourist who expects everyone to speak English; the arrogant patriot who thinks every country in the world should pattern itself after the United States; the drunken reveler who sees the anonymity of traveling abroad as an opportunity to drop all civilized inhibitions; the rich American who lives like the stars of movies, soap operas, and pulp fiction; the spoiled and pampered teenager with the carefree life-style—all have contributed to the development of these misleading but nevertheless convincing images in the eyes of those who may not have had much experience with other, more typical Americans.

More seasoned images of Americans might include some or all of the following characteristics. Americans are said to be

- Outgoing and friendly

- Informal

- Loud, rude, boastful

- Immature

- Hard working

- Extravagant and wasteful

- Sure they have all the answers

- Lacking in class consciousness and disrespectful of authority

- Racially prejudiced

- Ignorant of other countries

- Wealthy

- Generous

- Promiscuous

- Always in a hurry.

While every stereotype contains a grain of truth, it is obvious when we consider individual differences that few American fit all or even most of the above descriptions. Nevertheless, it may be initially impossible for U.S. students to avoid being nationally typecast. Nor, when they are, will it be much fun for them to have to throw off these roles and assumptions. The challenge is to try to behave in a manner that will convince local hosts that the stereotype does not quite fit.

It may seem a bit contradictory to suggest that because of the unique social and cultural milieu of the United States, most Americans tend to be less reserved, less inhibited, and less restrained than others in their efforts to communicate friendliness and sociability. But in some areas of the world this outgoing manner, especially on the part of young women, can be grossly misinterpreted. A friendly smile and a warm "hello" on the streets of Rome could easily be interpreted by an Italian man as something more than mere friendliness.

Until one develops a feel for the social characteristics of the area in which one is living and studying, it is wise to be somewhat formal and restrained in social contacts. By the same token, American students should not expect the local populace to welcome them immediately or with open arms. It is useful to keep in mind that formality and restraint are not necessarily an expression of unfriendliness but may simply be characteristic of indigenous social manners.

Because the United States is a world leader that exerts a great deal of power and influence in the international political arena, some citizens of other nations may be resentful of Americans, particularly if they do not agree with U.S. policies. Occasionally, resentment toward U.S. foreign policy may be directed toward U.S. students overseas. Students may not be able to do much about that state of affairs, but they should try to understand the origins of the attitudes and not take them personally. U.S. students traveling abroad should also be sensitive to the relative prosperity of the United States and to the fact that many people, particularly in the developing world, may be envious of the material wealth and opportunities available to U.S. citizens.

FITTING IN

Social customs differ greatly from one country to another. It is therefore impossible here to give guidelines that will be applicable for U.S. students in every culture. Generally speaking, your daughter can be herself as long as she remains courteous and dignified. As an outsider, erring on the side of being respectful will produce allowances for the things not immediately understood or fully accepted. As a guest in someone else's country, she should behave pretty much in the same manner as she would if she were a guest in someone's home. On the other hand, she will feel a great desire to fit in, to put guest status behind her, and to live and act like a native. Accomplishing this often requires learning new behaviors and adapting to different social and cultural values.

Social customs differ from one country and culture to another, and there is simply no way students can fit in and feel at home unless they learn what is and is not appropriate behavior. Students should expect things to be different overseas. For guidance, they should know that it is seldom inappropriate for a stranger to inquire politely about local customs and social niceties. This will help carry them through to the time when life returns to normal, a "new normal" in which they feel comfortable in their new surroundings.

BEING A YOUNG AMERICAN WOMAN OVERSEAS

Some American women have a hard time adjusting to attitudes they encounter abroad in public and private interactions between men and women. It is not uncommon to be honked at, stared at, verbally and loudly appraised, and to be actively noticed simply for being an American woman. Indigenous women, who often get the same sort of treatment, have been taught how to ignore, or at least not be equally offended by, the attention.

Eye contact between strangers or a feminine smile at someone passing in the street may result in totally unexpected invitations. Some women feel they are forced to stare intently at the ground while they walk down the street. (In some countries, young, unmarried women do not walk in public alone.) From some local perspectives, all western women are considered promiscuous, and the cultural misunderstandings that come out of this image can lead to difficult and unpleasant experiences. Other misleading assumptions and stereotypes exist as well, on all sides.

The only remedy for U.S. students is to learn the unwritten rules as quickly as possible and to act accordingly. That does not necessarily mean adopting all indigenous attitudes and behaviors. It does mean being aware of the responses certain behaviors are likely to produce in others. Depending on the circumstances of the program, women can usually provide support for each other. Former students suggest that getting together several times early in the stay to talk about what works and what doesn't is very helpful, especially for dealing with unwanted male attention. Obviously, making friends with local women is also a very fundamental way of finding comfortable ground.

Needless to say, this special and surprising status may make male-female friendships more difficult to develop. Women need to be careful about the implicit messages they may be communicating, however unintentionally. Above all, they need to try to maintain the perspective that these challenging and sometimes difficult experiences are part of the growth of cultural understanding that is one of the important reasons for studying abroad. The key lies in trying to understand in advance not only the gender roles and assumptions that may prevail elsewhere, but also the uniqueness of American sexual politics, which may or may not be understood, much less have a place, in other countries.

RACIAL AND ETHNIC CONCERNS

No two students studying abroad ever have quite the same experience, even in the same program and country. This is true for students from U.S. minority backgrounds. Reports from past participants vary from those who felt exhilarated to be free of the pressure of American race relations, to those who experienced different degrees of innocent curiosity about their ethnicity, to those who felt they met both familiar and new types of ostracism and prejudice and had to learn new coping strategies. But very few minority students who have studied abroad conclude that the racial or ethnic problems that can be encountered in other countries represent sufficient reasons for not going.

Some such students of course study abroad in part to seek a deeper understanding of their cultural heritage. Thus, students with a heritage in Africa may head to Zimbabwe, Ghana, or Kenya, while students with a Latin American background may head for the Dominican Republic, Mexico, or Chile. Most find many connections with aspects of their family background and upbringing. But they also discover that they are much more American than they had imagined, and they are often seen this way by the natives of the country in which they study.

Minority students who study abroad do so for reasons as diverse as those that attract other U.S. students. In some countries, such as England or Brazil, they find as much cultural diversity as exists in the United States, along with quite different and often liberating attitudes toward that diversity. In other countries, of course, they find they stand out as cultural curiosities, which may or may not be accompanied by degrees of exclusion or overt social prejudice.

Such students often find that study abroad helps them clarify lines between their personal, American, and ethnic or racial identity. On the other hand, they advise fellow students to know what they are getting into and prepare for it. This process needs to begin on the home campus, by finding students of similar background who have studied abroad, ideally in the same location. Many overseas programs pay special attention to questions of inclusion and diversity, providing students with special orientation and counselling services. Parents and students are perfectly justified in asking beforehand about any prejudices and social attitudes that might exist overseas to make life uncomfortable for their children, and how the program will deal with the situation.

Here are some things students can do during their study abroad program to explore career options and enhance their future prospects.

- Maintain a notebook of contacts. Include the name, address, phone number, and e-mail address of every interesting professional you meet.

- Contact alumni. Meet them at their place of business or socially. Express your interest in staying on after your program of study ends, or your interest in returning after graduation.

- Look for schools that teach in English. What qualifications do their teachers have?

- If in a home stay, talk with adults in the family about the local economy. Take every opportunity to meet the family's friends and extended family, to network.

- Practice, practice, practice the local language. If the language is English, learn the idioms, accent, vocabulary, etc. Speak with natives in all walks of life, constantly. Read the local and national papers and periodicals.

- When you encounter older Americans living locally, introduce yourself. Make note of where they are employed and how they obtained their positions.

- Pay attention to the cost of living, as opposed to that of the United States. Figure out how much money you would need to live there.

- Have a friend at home pick up and save summer job and internship information for you.

- If graduate study in the host country might be an option, get application information while you're there.

Adapted from a checklist prepared by Amherst College.

BEING GAY, LESBIAN, OR BISEXUAL ABROAD

It is important for gay, lesbian, and bisexual students to be aware of laws pertaining to homosexuality in other countries, as well as the general attitudes of the populace toward homosexual foreigners. Overall, the countries visited may be more or less tolerant than the United States. Moreover, as in the United States, regardless of general attitudes and laws, there are likely to be pockets of intolerance. Country-specific information is often available from campus offices, personnel, and student groups. Students should talk with other students who have gone before them.

For information on issues and resources pertaining to gay, lesbian, and bisexual travel, students may want to consult publications available in bookstores and libraries that carry literature such as *Gaia's Guide,* "an international guide for traveling women," that includes information on restaurants, accommodations, travel, and the like; or *Sparticus International Gay Guide,* which provides listings of hotlines, publications, bars, etc. for gay men throughout the world.

Conclusion

The counsel and caution in this chapter should not be taken to suggest to parents that the worst is likely to happen to their son or daughter while overseas. Rather, it is meant to emphasize that overseas programs and their leaders are aware of the complexities, misunderstandings, ambiguities, and potential dangers involved in the process of living and learning in a foreign country and culture. Their aim is to make sure that students receive the very best advice and information on how to avoid or at least prepare for any situation that might arise, thereby maximizing the possibilities that the overseas study experience will be rich and bountiful, healthy and safe. There are always risks and ups and downs, and not every program or location works equally well for every participant, but it is highly likely that your son or daughter will make the necessary adjustments, enjoy nearly every day for the interest and adventure it brings, and find out, suddenly, before he or she is ready for it, that it is time to think about, and then in fact to begin, the journey home.

□   □   □

Part 6

Coming Home

For most students the time spent studying abroad passes very quickly, especially after they have settled in and become comfortable in their new surroundings. For others, time overseas has an "unreal" feel about it, since the American markers for the passing of time are replaced by foreign ones—different daily routines for eating, sleeping, learning, relaxing, even sometimes a different cultural valuation of the meaning of time itself. A few students count the passing days until their program ends, but they are the exceptions.

During this period, whether less than a month or an entire year, students may or may not have been in regular contact with parents, friends, and campus advisers. They may have received all sorts of information on what has occurred during their absence, or they may have been quite out of touch, either by choice or because of the distances and circumstances involved. Contacts with home are welcome almost always, and of course remind students that what they are experiencing is a finite sojourn, not the beginning of the rest of their life.

Like all good things, however, the study abroad experience, whatever its duration, ends and students return home. While they invariably look with eagerness to the moment when they will be back on American soil, most also want to hold on to the richness of their overseas experience for as long as possible, and many begin immediately to make plans to return. As suggested throughout this book, living and learning on overseas soil usually brings unanticipated dimensions of intellectual and personal maturity, independence, and an invigorated sense of direction and involvement. Besides this, students invariably report, it is fun!

But, whereas for parents the safe homecoming of a daughter or son may primarily elicit feelings of relief and happiness, students themselves often harbor a complex of new feelings and attitudes, not all of which are positive. When these new feelings and attitudes come up too quickly against the familiar realities of American social life and the responsibilities of being a campus-bound

U.S. student, of being home again, it is not unusual for them to undergo a short-lived period that experts in cross-cultural travel have termed "reverse culture shock."

Reverse Culture Shock

Like its antecedent, reverse culture shock is entirely normal, is seldom severe or long-lasting, and varies in its effects from student to student. It comes about when students realize that their overseas experience has now indeed ended and begin missing its most positive aspects. Obviously, longer periods of time away carry greater potential for the sort of transforming changes study abroad is capable of producing, but even shorter programs that successfully integrate students into a foreign culture can have a tremendous impact.

Some students are simply more adaptive than others and thus fit in quickly and smoothly at both ends of the spectrum, while others have trouble at both ends. Others—especially those on short-term study tours—may have identified so much with their American group and its experiences that they may not have truly entered a foreign culture, so the only loss they feel in coming home is the end of opportunities for travel and on-the-road camaraderie.

Reverse culture shock can have different manifestations at home and on campus. Most returnees report that readjusting to campus expectations and the campus culture is more difficult than adjusting to American life in general, so it is advisable for students to have some down time at home before classes begin again.

At its most extreme, however, reverse culture shock can include temporary symptoms such as physical and mental disorientation, feelings of alienation from family and friends, frustration over the absence of things they got used to overseas or with the familiar things they thought they had rejected, irritability at seemingly minor events and encounters, rejection of their own culture, boredom, and lack of direction. This is not to predict that any of this will happen to your daughter or son, only that if it does, it is likely to gain much of its strength for having been unanticipated. If it does, an awareness of its characteristics and commonness may help in dealing with its symptoms.

Experience suggests that most returned students have strongly positive memories of what they have seen and done. Even the difficult periods often get transformed in retrospect into "learning experiences." With the recognition that they have grown and changed, students face the inevitable sense of loss of the foreign environment in which that evolution occurred. Students who truly settled into the new culture often describe the adjustment as one of "having become myself again, only different." They will be aware that the sights and sounds, foods and habits, acquaintances and friends that formed their intense living and learning environment while abroad and became part of their daily consciousness are fading fast into memory.

Students in the throes of reverse culture shock often find that they seem to have little in common with their old friends; that beyond polite inquiries no one seems very interested in listening to them talk about their experiences abroad; that attitudes of family and friends seem parochial; and that there is seemingly no place to go with the knowledge and skills they feel they acquired abroad. Moreover, life at home and on the home campus often seems restrictive and unexciting.

They may also fear that no one will understand what they have lived at first hand or see the changes that have come about in their outlook. Thus, while glad to be home again, students may hesitate to resume the rhythms and values of American academic life. While such feelings may be vague and unformed, there may be a host of concerns over a variety of more pragmatic matters, such as getting into the appropriate courses for the next term, finding housing and roommates, and getting academic credit for what they have learned. Now that they are one step closer to graduation, many also have anxiety about the impact of their sojourn on career and other plans.

To some degree or another reverse culture shock is predictable. After all, most students will have matured and grown in self-reliance while abroad. They will have become accustomed to looking at the world through a different set of cultural glasses and know that doing so can result in new ways of thinking, feeling, talking, seeing. They will have met different types of people and had different kinds of conversations. They may have adjusted to a different pace of life or a different set of social norms. Students may come home dressing more fashionably, slurping their soup, or arriving late for appointments. But the real changes are likely to be internal.

There will be changes parents and friends will notice (e.g., in dress, manner, etc.) that returnees won't see. Other changes returnees will feel inside (e.g., intellectual, personal, political values); these will not be obvious on the outside and may take time to manifest themselves. Some of the changes will prove to be temporary; others will endure. Long after graduation, students who studied abroad report that the overseas experience had a greater impact on them than did anything else during their undergraduate years, but they recognize that something truly important has happened to them well before they finally decide what it means.

To help your son or daughter to get the most out of reverse culture shock, it is important to understand that the phases of reverse culture shock resemble those of the original phenomenon. Immediately upon arrival home, most returnees go through an initial stage of euphoria and excitement. Most are overwhelmed by the sheer joy and cultural comfort of being back on native turf. But as they try to settle back into their former routines, they recognize that their overseas experience has changed some of their previously held social perceptions and cultural assumptions, or even what it means to be themselves. Each has become, in a sense, a somewhat new person, or at least that is the way it feels. Some are not only proud of their growth and independence, but fearful of losing it as their former life once again surrounds them.

The intensity of these growing pains is usually rather short-lived, since home will never be as foreign as the foreign environment they adjusted to overseas. Also, students' experience of dealing successfully with culture shock abroad will have provided them with the psychological tools for dealing with the challenges of readjustment on native ground. Obviously, the more they have changed, the more difficult it will be to restore equilibrium. However, if you and they are aware of the changes and seek to learn from them, smooth adaptation is likely. The key is to find strategies that integrate the growth that has taken place into subsequent studies and career plans.

After the initial period of readjustment, most students who have studied abroad readjust rather rapidly to the familiar rhythms and routines of American academic life. The experience of learning within a different educational system and cultural environment has a liberating and confidence-building effect. Students frequently comment on how the overseas experience has helped them "learn how to learn" and take responsibility for their own education.

Many are quite eager to work hard and take advantage of the high quality of home-campus teaching and resources, something they admit they may not have fully appreciated previously. Campus advisers sometimes inform faculty of which students in their classes have been abroad and may have special expertise or perspectives to share in class. Faculty usually notice significant differences in the depths of their interests, knowledge, and motivation. Students, in turn, generally find ways to incorporate some of what they have learned into their current courses. Academically, returned study abroad students usually perform at a higher level of achievement, and their grades tend to reflect this.

Reentry Programming

Some students will have had the benefit of an overseas reentry program in the host country to discuss and prepare for coming home. Most will not. They will have said their farewells, hopped on a plane, and landed back in the States, where many campuses will offer some sort of reentry program. These vary from a one- or two-day retreat to an afternoon or evening social occasion. Reentry programs give students a chance to compare and contrast their experiences and to begin new friendships with others who have had an overseas experience.

Students are encouraged in reentry sessions to maintain contact with friends they made overseas, foreign and American, and to remain in touch with the culture they entered and now have left.

Remembering what it was like to have been, for a time, a foreigner often inspires returned students to try to get to know the international students on their campus or others from minority backgrounds who may themselves be feeling some of the same social dislocation and alienation they felt when they were overseas. The key, they will be told, is to build on the cross-cultural coping skills they now possess and to find conscious ways of integrating their new self into their evolving personal and academic life, rather than seeing it as a dream or something irrelevant to their future.

Securing Academic Credit and Resuming Studies

In most instances, if your daughter or son has done all that was required and requested before departure, there should be few if any difficulties in receiving anticipated (and preapproved) course credits. This, however, assumes that all of the following are true:

- That the courses taken were the ones that were preapproved, or if changes were made, that the substitutions were approved

- That performance in the classes taken was of a passing standard

- That for any work that was only conditionally preapproved or that is being transferred in from programs not directly sponsored by the home campus complete records were kept of all work done abroad (papers, exams, journals, and the like) for campus review by faculty or others responsible for granting credit

- That any official transcripts and other records expected from overseas institutions, or from the U.S. college, university, or agency that sponsored the program, arrive and are processed quickly by the registrar's office

- That preregistration for the coming term was done in advance from overseas.

If the above conditions have been met, then signing up for new courses and getting back into the U.S. academic mainstream ought to be relatively easy. If they have not, students will have to deal with the frustration of not knowing exactly where things stand with regard to credit. This in turn can affect their registration for on-going course work, especially if courses taken overseas are prerequisites for other courses they now wish to take. It is not uncommon for study abroad credits not to be posted on the home transcript until months after the student has returned to the United States, generally because many universities abroad take longer than U.S. institutions to process grades and because conversions may have to be done to convert the grades and credits into their

U.S. equivalents. The study abroad office on the home campus usually can tell a student approximately when transcripts will arrive or help a student follow up if they are unusually late.

Program Evaluation

Upon their return to campus, students are usually asked to complete a written evaluation of their study abroad program. These evaluations are extremely useful for future participants and are consulted frequently by faculty and staff. Copies of the forms are also mailed to the program sponsors and on-site directors. Frequently, program changes are made in response to students' comments. The experience of filling out the questionnaire also gives returnees the chance to reflect on what they have been through and their many achievements, and it provides some additional closure on the experience.

Campuses that have been involved in study abroad for many years attempt to distinguish between those educational impacts that can be attributed to the structures, values, and personnel of a given program per se, from the individual growth that occurs due to personal student initiative, the foreign cultural environment in general, or serendipity.

Building on the Experience

Once students have been welcomed home, completed their evaluations, and resumed their normal studies, there is a strong temptation to view the cycle as complete. Often, however, the lingering impact of having been abroad remains very strong, and students feel a need to find outlets for it. Returned study abroad students are encouraged to continue their own learning by doing some of the following:

■ Becoming involved in campus-based international activities such as serving as a host, roommate, or tutor for an international student or joining an international club

■ Acting as peer counselors to help other students understand why studying abroad is important and help them select the program that best serves their interests

■ Volunteering to talk about the country where they lived in local elementary schools

■ Leading orientation sessions to prepare departing students for the experience ahead

■ Joining international organizations

- Participating in international outreach activities on campus and in the community (e.g., speakers bureaus, international symposia, photo contests)

- Keeping alive the language they learned overseas by living in language houses and participating in conversation circles

- Pursuing graduate fellowships, scholarships, and work abroad opportunities.

Career Planning

A large percentage of returned study abroad students make a beeline for the campus career center. Their hope is to make use of what they have learned abroad in a quest for an international career, or at least one that allows them to travel, building on their knowledge of the language and culture of the country where they have studied. Even today, some career offices have little experience working with students who wish to exploit what they learned on a study-abroad program, though they generally try to do what they can to help. Others are very able to assist such students, having ample international career resources and contact with employers looking to hire students with this background. They are delighted to see such students and will do everything in their power to provide pragmatic counsel.

In either case, students will still have to show some of the same initiative that led them to study abroad in the first place. A short list of things students can and should do might include the following:

- With the help of career center staff, prepare a resume. Make sure it adequately describes the experience abroad and all cross-cultural adaptation skills, including language competency.

- Learn about the full range of services for job-hunting seniors that are offered by the career center.

- Attend all relevant job-seekers' workshops.

- Learn whether firms with offices abroad recruit on campus. Don't be distressed to learn that one might have to work in the United States first.

- Ascertain whether a higher degree is needed to obtain the desired position. What graduate entrance exams are required? Where in the United States or abroad can that degree be earned?

- Make time to gather and pursue short-term and permanent work-abroad resources.

- Keep in touch with contacts gathered abroad. Write to them, stating serious interest in returning to work after graduation.

- Investigate short-session programs that offer instruction in the teaching of English as a second language. Do they help with job placement?

- Determine your financial situation. Must you earn some short-term support money before you go? How long can you afford to live abroad?

Giving Students the Final Word

There are many ways to study abroad and many responses to the experience, some of which are reflected in the student quotations with which we end this book. If these seem to be carefully selected (and selective) responses, please understand that anyone who has listened to study abroad returnees will find in what these few students say and how they say it echoes of common belief in the value of what they have done.

"I cannot accurately describe on paper everything that this experience has done for me. The semester was absolutely amazing, irreplaceable, and the best decision I've ever made in my entire life. The personal growth and development and self-discovery that one goes through are worth every penny."

"A time abroad is vital to a sincere and far-reaching exploration of one's own self. In particular, you discover the limits of your patience, who can be blamed for failures, and to what degree you can create successful situations. You develop self-reliance and build your own strengths in facing fear-inducing situations and especially, you realize the value of your own family, your culture, your background and experiences."

"This was one of the best experiences of my life, and I urge anyone and everyone to do it. It opened up a whole new world that one can only see by traveling and being on one's own."

"When I was in France as an adolescent, I was always an outsider looking into the French way of life, constantly surrounded by my native language and American environment. This time, however, I took a different approach which consequently led to my personal growth and development. I made an effort to merge with the culture. This was accomplished by attending a French institution, playing soccer on a French team, living with a French woman, and attending cultural events to get a sense of French history. Through full-immersion, I believe I have truly discovered French culture and life."

"I should have gone for a year. One semester was not enough."

"The experiences gained from study abroad are far greater than just academic. They can benefit any student in building confidence, independence, and a better understanding of the world."

"Brazil has so much to offer, both in natural resources and in culture; no textbook or classroom lecture can do justice to either. Discovering and experiencing things first hand is exciting, convincing, and longer-lasting than hearing about things from others."

"The opportunity is precious; one can scarcely avoid an intensive cultural experience. The amount of learning and growth sparked by work and life in Bodh Gaya is astronomical. The beauty of realizing the similarities shared by vastly different cultures and the resiliency of the human spirit is one inexpressible treasure offered by this program."

"Although I had a lot of fun in Japan, I also worked harder than ever before. It was satisfying because it was so hard. Just getting through the day, dealing with the language and the crowds—I felt proud of the accomplishment. I made a lot of sacrifices by leaving the United States for a year, but the benefits were huge. I have this feeling now, after surviving that year, that scholastically I can pretty much handle any challenge."

"My overall experience was great. It actually made me more independent and studious. I also truly experienced how the Chinese live, and I made life-long friends. The best thing is to be open and courageous. Take the bus and ride the subway, and don't worry about what they will think of you. They expect you to be weird."

"After my time in Ecuador, I understand to a greater degree that relationships are more important than schedules. I understand that we, North Americans, can't go into Latin America to change it. It won't work. We must go in to learn and maybe lend a helping hand, but we must let them make the decisions. One of the best and most difficult parts of the program was living with an Ecuadorian family. Students should know ahead of time that it will be tough, but the insights gained make this experience well worth it."

"This was honestly one of the most incredible years of my life. My academic experience far exceeded my expectations and I grew a lot personally. My Hebrew definitely improved by leaps and bounds, although I am far from fluent. I had to get used to living in a completely new environment. It was a crazy year to be there because of the multiple bombings, Rabin's assassination, and the elections. Even though there were some stressful moments, I am very glad I was there for everything. It really made me feel closer to the country and the people."

"My study abroad experience was something that has touched my life and changed it in a positive way. I learned not only about Japan, its people, its language, and its culture, but more importantly, I learned about myself and my own country."

"Studying in Mexico was an unbelievable experience. I learned to speak Spanish and had fun at the same time. The people were nice and patient, and the country was beautiful. It was hard to come home. When everyone came to say goodbye, they said, "Don't go. Do you have to go? Can you change your ticket?""

"I only miss the Indonesian people, the food, the climate, the classes, and the teachers. When can I go back?"

□ □ □